Lean Manufacturing
for the Small Shop

Lean Manufacturing for the Small Shop

Gary Conner

Society of Manufacturing Engineers
Dearborn, Michigan

Library of Congress Catalog Card Number: 00-134042
International Standard Book Number: 0-87263-520-1

Additional copies may be obtained by contacting:
Society of Manufacturing Engineers
Customer Service
One SME Drive, P.O. Box 930
Dearborn, Michigan 48121
1-800-733-4763
www.sme.org **Coventry University**

SME staff who participated in producing this book:

Phillip Mitchell, Senior Editor
Rosemary Csizmadia, Production Supervisor
Frances Kania, Production Assistant
Kathye Quirk, Graphic Designer/Cover Design
Printed in the United States of America

To my Creator, for the breath of life...
to ~~Pamela~~, for taking my breath away.

ISHA

Acknowledgements

Robert Donnelly of Contact Lumber, Portland, Oregon. For his unparalleled respect for learning, and for his unending dedication to the concepts and principles of continuous improvement. I was privileged to know him for only two short years, but I will be influenced by his energy for the rest of my life.

Tom Nielsen of Nielsen Manufacturing, Inc., Salem, Oregon. For the opportunity to challenge my own capabilities, for showing me the value of looking inward for opportunities and solutions. And for the ultimate honor an employer can bestow on an employee, enfranchisement to fully participate.

To **David Dixon** of Technical Change Associates, Ogden, Utah, for affording me the chance to work with some remarkable companies, and for allowing me to share the Lean Manufacturing Principles with some unforgettable people.

Table of Contents

Preface

There has been a wealth of information written on the subject of the Toyota production system, most of it based on and directed toward larger organizations. This book will describe a set of proven steps necessary to implement the Lean approach within a job shop environment. This book has been written primarily for the person charged with implementing Lean in a small- to medium-sized organization who may not be able to afford expensive consultant fees.

Obviously, there are major differences between the business realities of an Original Equipment Manufacturer (OEM) and a job shop. To overlay a template from Toyota or Ford Motor Company and expect it to work in a job shop dealing with thousands of part numbers, with little or no forecasting, is not reasonable.

How can a small company hope to be Lean while at the same time remaining flexible? The mental model of a Lean enterprise vehicle referred to throughout this book, and the recurring theme of applying a hybrid approach and model line, are meant to highlight the potential for capitalizing on the similarities while acknowledging the differences between the OEM and the job shop environment.

USING A MEASURE OF FAITH

I am writing this as I sit in the terminal of the St. Louis Airport, just having been to a revival meeting of sorts. A Lean conference, "The Best in North America," held just a short walk from the famous St. Louis Arch, has for the past few days provided a chance to interface with many other Lean practitioners. Hundreds of attendees were here to either benchmark their progress or test their strategy against the other approaches. They were exchanging ideas, teaching others, exploring expansion opportunities, or simply looking for ways to mature their own performance. They came from all over the United States to learn how best to plan and implement the Lean enterprise principles. Others were here simply to gather information about the Lean approach, enabling themselves through training. It was heartwarming to recognize the level of effort and to see how many others were working hard to get better every day.

I have been at the Lean process for nearly 20 years. It was a humbling experience to watch and listen to representatives from newly converted companies at this conference. It was encouraging to listen to them describe the challenges and changes, hearing the pride in their voices as they described a particular success. I also saw them grimacing over the agony of a less than perfect attempt. I could not help but sympathize with their pain or empathize with their elation.

The success stories fill my sails with wind, revitalize me as a disciple of change. They recharge my batteries and ready me to go back home and try again. But it also helps to hear of the failures, because a warning is as good as a lesson learned the hard way. It is less likely that miscues or backsliding will take place if you have gathered a few good horror stories describing someone else's flop.

I call this conference a revival meeting because I can't help but notice many similarities between the implementation of the Lean approach and the adoption of a new faith or religion. Each journey requires a measure of faith. It may not have an explicit start and finish point. Long-range vision is required, and at times, the process demands much time and energy. It is a never-ending process of improvement and cultural change. Exhilarating one moment, disheartening the next.

Like the transformation of someone adopting Lean, a person changing his/her faith may spend years in research, devoting hours, weeks, or months to contemplation and meaningful meditation about how best to apply the new knowledge to his/her life. It would not be surprising to see this person applying thoughtful attention to volumes of information and modifying lifelong behaviors or long-held beliefs and values. Certainly this is no easy matter and can be one of the most significant and challenging decisions in a person's life.

To change a person's religion often means to challenge the very foundation upon which a family has been built. In the exuberance of his newfound faith, a convert may drive away loved ones. When only one or two persons in the family embrace a new belief system, the stress of change can result in disagreement, division, or even dysfunction. The person may be ostracized or even cast out by family members. This can happen in companies adopting the Lean approach as well. Companies may have one or two converts who recognize the truth or value of the Lean approach, while others see no need to change, sometimes even becoming a source of discouragement for the new disciples.

The effort required to overcome discouragement, the normal tendency to backslide, the potential for hindrance from nonbelievers, and the fact that many around the person may not share his values and views create a constant need for support. These are the same reasons churches conduct revival meetings. Those adopting Lean as a way of life also need much study, communication, reciprocal visits, and dialog between fellow believers.

For me, the many similarities between the adoption of Lean and a conversion of faith demonstrate the importance of conferences such as "The Best of North America." Talking about "the way" serves to bolster the faith of each adherent. All of us attending gain a renewed energy and are bolstered from within to carry ourselves toward the next milestone in our journey. And we recognize that we are not alone. This may be the most powerful message communicated at these events. We find others with whom we can network and it helps our commitment to keep working toward the goal of "perfection," which, in this case, is waste-free manufacturing. Like a spiritual goal, perfection is not easily attainable. We would like to be better than we are, but somehow we always have trouble meeting the ideal. Nonetheless, we realize that there is no other way, so we keep at it. Much like the nonstop attempts to perfect faith, each of us trying to adopt the Lean way realizes that the goal of perfection is often just out of reach. But again, we know the alternative is not an acceptable option, so we press on. Getting together to encourage one another is somehow very therapeutic.

Survival in the marketplace is dependent on adhering as closely as possible to the principles of Lean. Perfection may be out of reach, but once in a while we see progress, a small success, a glimmer of what it could be like in paradise. That goal, that vision, that glimmer is what keeps us on the path.

MY HEROES HAVE ALWAYS BEEN MECHANICS

I have always had great admiration for the skill and patience of good mechanics, especially those who can take an engine completely apart and put it back together; the ones who have all the tools and know how to use them. They love the machine, and they treat it with healthy respect. Fully aware of the danger, they are equally aware of the potential for power. They understand and have learned to bridle the inert energies lying dormant in the components assembled into an automobile engine, all waiting to be unleashed in precisely measured quantities of fuel, air, and electricity. Power exploding within metallic cylinders is transformed into controlled force, harnessed and transferred from engine to clutch, from transmission to drive lines, and finally transmitted to wheels and tires and then to the road in the form of torque.

I have always wanted to be able to build a high-performance engine from the ground up, but unfortunately, I do not have the knowledge or skills to do it. I do not possess the correct set of tools in my garage either. It's not that I am incapable of learning to be a skilled mechanic. If I had someone to teach me, and time to learn, I know that I am capable. I have a basic set of tools and can perform basic repairs. However, it is not just a matter of my time. I would really need the time of a skilled person to teach me as well. Haphazardly approaching a project such as engine rebuilding without the correct tools or skills could be pretty expensive, time-consuming, and possibly life threatening if I were to make a serious mistake.

So, I will probably never be an automobile mechanic. But for the past few years, I have had the rare opportunity to do another kind of engine rebuilding. Not automobile engines, but the engines of industry: manufacturing firms. Because of my extensive experience in helping to design and implement manufacturing work cells and fast setup projects, companies started asking me to help them. It started on an informal basis. But, before I knew it, I was working full time as a consultant. Without having a plan to do so, I came to realize that I had become a mechanic of sorts. Over time, I had obtained a set of tools that others needed. I had gathered methods and timesaving techniques that companies needed to apply to the rebuilding of their engines.

I have had the honor of working with some of the best change agents in the business. Under their tutelage, I have expanded my knowledge to areas in virtually every industry. They have taught me well, as have the authors listed in the bibliography. I have tried to read nearly every book published on the subject of Just-in-Time, world-class manufacturing, and the Lean approach. This, coupled with hands-on experience, has served me well.

I have worked with more than 40 companies across the United States. The majority of these companies have been small- to medium-sized organizations, from a mom-and-pop shop in the little town of Independence, Oregon, with 10 people, to shops in Chicago, Illinois, with 1,200 people, and every size in between. I have worked on projects as simple as training teams how to get along and as complicated as an entire facilities layout and cellularization for a precision sheet metal company of 300 people.

By writing this book, I hope to share experiences, ideas, tools, and case studies that can help you and your company become qualified mechanics of Lean. My primary motivation is not to convince anyone to adopt Lean. There are many well-written books on that subject and I refer to them often in this book. My assumption is that if you are reading this, you already know that you need to convert to Lean. My hope is to share some tools to make the transition easier for small- and medium-sized companies, and to ensure that the method of implementation provides long-lasting gains.

You may contact me at the following address, phone number, or e-mail address.

Gary Conner
Lean Enterprise Training
P.O. Box 381
Prineville, OR 97754
Telephone: 541-923-6241
e-mail: Lean1mfg@aol.com
website: http://www.leanenterprise.bizland.com

1

It's About Time

Yes, it is about time. You may think this is a strange beginning, but the title of this chapter has a double meaning because I am addressing two issues.

First, managing a company using the *Lean* approach requires everybody at every level of the organization to think about time all the time. Efficient use of time has been said to be one of the greatest indicators of competitiveness.

Second, it's about time the Lean approach was directed to small businesses! For too long, written material about the Lean approach, about world-class manufacturing, about Just-in-Time (JIT), about cellularization, has been directed to the Original Equipment Manufacturers (OEMs). There is no shortage of case studies, examples, and literature describing the steps. Huge companies such as the Ford Motor Company or General Electric have adopted the Lean mentality. But what about the little guy? What about the 100-person shop, or the 10-person shop? Or, what about the mom-and-pop shop that has for years been taking care of its customers, and because of its high quality, low cost, and impeccable service, is now faced with unparalleled growth?

Recent surveys conducted by the Small Business Administration (SBA) show that over 99 percent of all manufacturing businesses in America employ less than 500 people, as shown in Table 1-1. The vast majority of these are not OEMs. They are suppliers, mom-and-pop shops, or what are known as job shops.

Allow me to define what I mean by the term *job shop*, since it is key the to rest of this book. I consider a job shop to be any operation not in the business of long run, proprietary, consistent, one-of-a-kind products. It also can be an organization serving one or two customers. Job shops would generally be smaller, "make-to-order" operations, very much like a restaurant. A savvy

Table 1-1. Number of people employed in manufacturing firms*

Number of People Employed	Number of Businesses	Percent
0-4	130,046	39
5-9	61,167	18
10-19	62,897	19
20-99	67,057	19
100-499	16,475	4
500+	4,923	1
Total	342,565	100

*Source: Small Business Administration, 1996

restaurateur would never have the chef cook one thousand steaks ahead of time just because that's how many the restaurant sells in a month. The chef would cook a steak to order, only after the order was placed. This is how job shops operate. They seldom build to stock. They most likely have less than two hundred employees at any one site.

Job shops do not make the same product every day. They may be suppliers to as few as 50 or to more than 200 different customers. Their business is likely "make to order," with thousands of part numbers, and they can never accurately predict which part number will get the call today or tomorrow.

So, once again, it's about time somebody talks to these smaller companies. That is what I intend to do in this book. I will discuss the concept of time as a once-spent, unrecoverable resource, and I will send the long-overdue message to non-OEM manufacturers and service organizations—to job shops—that Lean enterprise techniques can also work for them.

This is not to say that the principles and case studies described in this book do not apply to OEM organizations. The techniques and examples are mutually beneficial to either large or small organizations.

But trying to apply the same tools in the same sequence or overlaying the same template to a job shop that you might implement at an assembly facility or an auto plant is shortsighted and generally foolish. Ignoring the need for job shop flexibility can slow down the process within an environment that should take advantage of the nimble nature of being small.

Trying to force-fit an OEM solution onto a job shop can have a negative and opposite effect on desired productivity results. Learning to recognize and apply the appropriate tools quickly, and to find where the greatest gains can be captured, will be the recurring theme of this book. It comes back to the same thing: it's about time.

TRADING TIME FOR DOLLARS

We all trade time for dollars, whether we are CEOs, managers, employees, or suppliers. Each of us in the process is trying to control, and at the same time being controlled by, time. We all make poor decisions about how we consume this precious resource. The goal is to trade time for the greatest value we can get. The concept of *value-added* is key to this principle. We are willing to pay someone for the time spent adding value, but we do not want to pay for the time spent adding no value, or what is called *non-value-added* activities.

What a precious and cherished possession time is! What a wonderful gift it would make if we could package it, wrap it up and give it to someone who desperately needs it. And yet, we spend it freely, we trade it away, we even waste it.

As infants, we do not have a concept of time. We eat when we are hungry, we sleep when we are tired. As we get a little older, we have to start paying attention to time. Schedules most often determined by someone else begin to develop into routines that shape our lives.

To young people, time seems to be an inexhaustible resource. We even wish it away as our 16th birthday approaches! "I would gladly trade the next three months of my life if I could just get my driver's license now. . ." Those same three months to a terminally ill person would seem an irreplaceable opportunity. So the importance of time can be viewed as relative to where we are in life.

The obscene—yes, obscene—waste of time is what this book will address. The Japanese call waste *muda*. For a very tangible example, think about garbage filling up and spilling out of a landfill.

We generate billions of tons of garbage and collect it in dumpsters, recycling centers, and landfills each year.

In a less tangible and less obvious sense, waste falls all around us every day and we walk right past it. If it stank, or somehow caused us physical discomfort, we might pay more attention. But, other than adding to the cost of everything we buy, we happily go about our daily activities, totally oblivious to the fact that we are often standing knee-deep in muda all day long.

How can we make the often invisible and obscene waste of most precious and nonrecyclable resources more visible, and therefore less likely to be taken for granted? If I can answer that question, showing how a systematic approach to Lean can be applied within the job shop environment, then I will have met my goal in writing this book.

Make versus Buy

The first challenge of every business is to convince someone to buy a product. But a customer can also be a competitor, possibly having the same equipment and capabilities to make the product we would like to supply. And of course, there is always someone else waiting on his front doorstep, quite happy to make the product for him if we cannot meet his needs for price, quality, or service.

The choice is always there, and if the criteria of three critical make-versus-buy decision drivers are not met, the choice ends up costing the business. What are the three key drivers in this decision-making process? Nothing earthshattering here. They are, and always have been, *cost*, *quality*, and *availability* (delivery).

As consumers, we make similar decisions almost every day. For example, many of us today have breadmakers. If the quality of bread is important to us, we may decide to make it ourselves rather than buy it from the bakery. If, on the other hand, we need bread right now and the time needed to make it is four hours, then we might make a buying decision (even if we will not be as happy with the quality). If the cost of raw materials (yeast, flour, eggs) becomes unacceptable, we may also prefer the buy-versus-make choice, since the bakery can leverage the buying power of a business that uses tons of flour rather than pounds.

The point is that all of us make the same kinds of make-versus-buy choices all the time. This includes our customers. We need to create an environment that makes it impossible for our customer to be as satisfied with any other choice as he or she is with us.

EVOLUTION OF A COMPANY

Companies with $60 million in annual sales did not start overnight at that sales rate. The beginnings are usually small and undramatic, in someone's garage or a rented warehouse. Operating on a shoestring budget, looking at each customer more as a bag of groceries than a future partner, the company grows in fits and jerks. It may take years or even decades. The result is more of a business "evolution" than a business "revolution."

If the business can make it through the first three to five years, if it takes good care of the customers it has, and if it focuses on the three decision drivers (cost, quality, delivery), then it is almost certain that the customer will ask for more. The company's reputation will spread by word of mouth, and other customers will seek the product as well. This will lead to capacity problems impeding its ability to meet the demand.

Next step: expansion. Now, the company can begin to both succeed and fail. What generally happens is that the moment of expansion comes well after the need for growth has passed. Everybody has been working mega-overtime, fuses are short, employees are screaming for a day off, you have missed a due date or two, and the customer is questioning whether he can rely on your capabilities. There is no time to think about the ideal method of adding capacity.

"Ready—Fire—Aim! Get some capacity in the door, do whatever you have to do! Wherever you have to put it! Just put it next to that other machine! Bob can run both machines! Call it Department XYZ! Start finding equipment for Department ABC! Start looking for a second building! Truck the material from Department XYZ to Department ABC!"

Ideally, a methodical plan of action would be drawn up as growth is required. Decisions would be based on the principles of the Lean enterprise. However, we know that conditions are not easy to foresee. Similarly, growth opportunity drops in our lap so unexpectedly we do not have the luxury of time to allow the ideal application of world-class techniques. This happens over and over.

Good things happen to good people. The sales team comes in with the great news, everybody slaps each other on the back, and the next day reality sets in. The need for growth becomes more like a fire to fight instead of something to celebrate. Success can seem to be the worst thing that ever happened. Time becomes the enemy, since it is in the shortest supply at the precise moment we need it the most, and the one thing we can't go out and buy. So, in the heat of battle we often must generate new policies and practices that will cost us for all time—unless we are disciplined enough to rethink the approach after the battle is over.

What creates the greatest long-term risk is that most companies never take the time to undo the damage of poor decisions made in the haste of battle. The company that will survive is the one led by visionaries who can look into the mirror of Lean technologies and recognize the opportunity to undo the damage sustained in the heat of a firefight.

Happily, the damage is very seldom irreparable. Through the tools, techniques, and case studies described in this book, I will demonstrate how companies from a wide variety of industries have been able to discover where mistakes of the past can be repaired, or prevented by either a major operation or a simple vaccine.

Every company is different and there is no "one size fits all." The tools are many and varied. I hope to introduce you to these tools in such a way that you can better select the correct ones and realize the real-life benefits from applying them to your organization. My goal is to develop a hunger within each reader to become a Lean mechanic.

The Beginning

Maybe you have done this: you walk to your corner grocery store and on the way you see a couple of youngsters sitting near a wall. In front of them is a cardboard box. Curious, you look in. Free puppies! You came for a gallon of milk. You leave with the memory of a gap-toothed smile from a future used-car salesman, a package of puppy chow, and a cute little ball of fur that will be the reason you begin subscribing to the newspaper.

What a great puppy! So willing, so thankful to be chosen, so eager to please! Not unlike the initial customer relationship with the mom-and-pop shop, right? "Come in early? No problem!" "Stay late? Glad to!" "How can we make your life better? We are so glad you chose us!"

But weeks later, that cute little puppy you brought home has grown. His legs are too long for his body and his tail is uncontrollable. He knocks over lamps and he chews through your favorite belt. He eats too much, makes too much noise, and runs for cover whenever a mess can possibly be blamed on him.

Again, the similarity between the mom-and-pop shop appears. Not a cute little puppy any more, not big enough to play with the big dogs yet, it is somewhere in the middle. Still wanting to please, but running for cover if about to be spanked for not following through on promises. I call this the teenage dog stage, and sooner or later every company passes through it. Just as with teenage dogs, it can be a difficult time of transition.

Responsibility comes with accountability, and what came easily at first now seems more complex and difficult to manage. The visual tool I use to describe this phenomenon is the "vertical versus horizontal" orientation graphic illustrated in this chapter. I will discuss this, but first, let me introduce you to Stan.

Stan works for AZTec, a company producing mainframe computers and industrial printers. Stan works in the sheet metal department and knows he is about to be laid off. The company wants to get out of the sheet metal business and concentrate on what it is really good at, which is designing, building, and installing circuit boards. Stan is considering his options. He talks to his boss and to the purchasing manager of sheet metal products, and convinces them that with his skill and abilities, he could become a supplier for the parts he used to make as an employee. Instead of taking a job with another company, he and his wife Fran decide to take funds from their retirement plan and start a small sheet metal business they call "The Jobbe Shoppe."

Stan and Fran clear out the pole barn used to store their boat and motor home. They go out to machine tool auctions and buy a small shear, a used CNC turret punch, a hydraulic press brake, a hardware press, and a spot-welder. Now Fran and Stan have an operation that might conceptually look like Figure 1-1. With sales

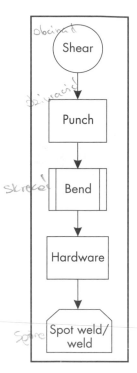

Figure 1-1. Stan and Fran's shop layout when first starting out.

commitments from his former employer, this expert machine tool operator has become a neo-phyte entrepreneur. Some variation of this story plays out every day of every month, in every city, state, and country on this planet.

If everything remains the same, then by default, what Stan and Fran have is a Lean system. There are no major sources of waste. Stan sets up his shop so that material can flow from one machine to the next in the logical order of processing it. Because Stan is an expert, there is no wasted material or unnecessary motion. When the machines need maintenance, Stan no doubt can perform this himself. When there is a quality problem, Stan would fix that too. He would never continue to make bad parts.

Because the shop is small, there is no place to store lots of material, so WIP (work-in-process) and FGI (finished goods inventory) levels are low. Inventory turns are high. Everything is good, and the customer is happy because Stan and Fran are always available if there is a need to communicate. There is no bureaucracy. Stan is an expert and the quality is exceptional. Due to their low overhead, costs are also kept to a minimum, allowing a positive buying decision for the customer.

But nothing ever stays the same. The customer now has a need to add new parts to the list Stan and Fran are making. But the new parts don't replace the parts currently being made. These will continue to be needed until the old version is phased out. Now, Dan comes in.

Dan was a buyer at AZTec who was downsized along with Stan and he moved over to AZTec's competitor, CorTEZ. Dan wants to buy the same type of product from Stan and Fran. This seems to be a very good thing, because now Fran can afford a new fax machine and Stan can get that new drill press he so badly needs. But before long, they can't keep up by themselves. So they hire a part-time student to help with the books and Stan hires his brother to run the equipment during the night to keep things going. Soon, there are five people on two shifts, all working as hard as they can to fill all the orders. Stan and Fran go down to the Small Business Administration to apply for a loan to build a larger shop and fill it with state-of-the-art equipment.

Stan is certainly learning a lot about running a business and while he is not an engineer, no one has to tell him that it makes perfect sense to put all the similar types of equipment together so that the operators can share tooling. It also allows them to have the most experienced employees close at hand to offer training and guidance to the new machine operators. After all, these are very expensive pieces of new equipment. The livelihood of all the employees and the future of the company are in the hands of a few knowledgeable people.

It is now 10 years later. Things look pretty much the same. Growth has been good. Every few years, Stan and Fran have made the pilgrimage to the machine tool manufacturing shows to see and shop for the latest and greatest machine. Everyone wants the machine that has all the bells and whistles, the one that can pump out a gazillion parts per hour. Now Stan and Fran's shop might look like Figure 1-2.

Stan and Fran now face a challenge. They have "horizontally" aligned their manufacturing processes as shown in Figure 1-3, so they have to provide inventory between each department to insure that no one runs out of work. Because the number of work orders (400 per month) is becoming hard to manage, they had to install a material resource planning/information management and job tracking system to tell them where any particular job is within the plant.

It is even more complicated, because Stan and Fran now need someone to direct each functional department. Departmental supervision becomes the personal goal of each operator in the plant. The way to be chosen is to make sure that every machine in the department is busy making parts all the time. However, even the best supervisor in the shop has a hard time keeping track of all 400 work orders. So instead of assisting the manufacturing teams, those hungry for advancement will spend hours learning to use the computer system to give the right answer in case someone asks about the status of a part. Add to this the cost of racking

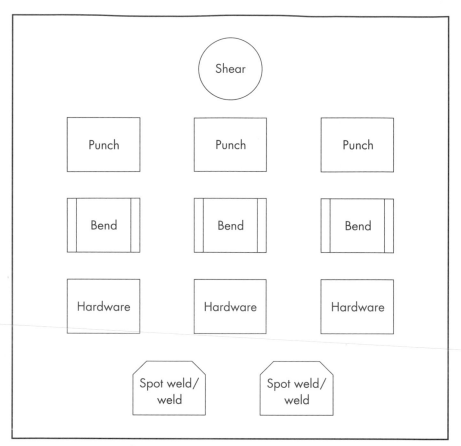

Figure 1-2. Stan and Fran's shop layout after growth.

systems to store all the material queued between the worksta-
tions, plus a forklift and drivers to move the material around, and
it's no wonder that Fran and Stan are beginning to wonder what
went wrong. When did it get so complicated?

The Lean approach would have us think about what made the
enterprise successful to begin with. The vertical integration of
processes that needed to be closely coupled is what originally made
the mom-and-pop shop so effective, as shown in Figure 1-4. Being
little and Lean is easy. Big and Lean is more difficult. How can we
return to or duplicate what worked in the beginning? If we can
answer that, we can be Lean again.

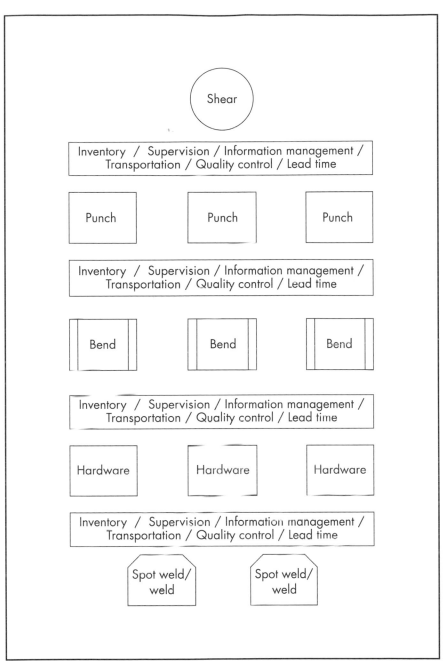

Figure 1-3. Stan and Fran's shop showing departmental layout with support systems.

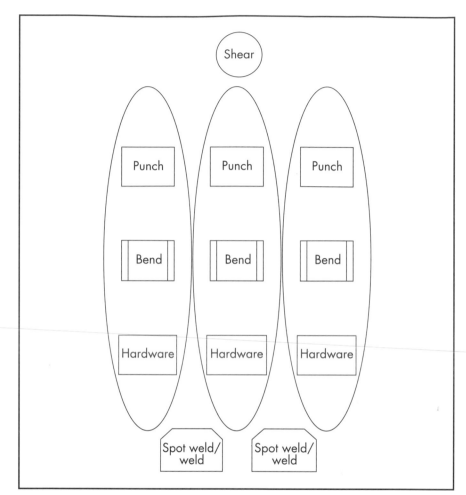

Figure 1-4. Stan and Fran's shop with vertically integrated layout.

Growth from Humble Beginnings

The scenario described earlier is not unique. Nearly every growing company goes through this, and it generally leads to the owners calling for help in identifying what can be done to turn around. It is a well-beaten path. Fran and Stan are not the first to travel down this road, and they are not alone. If you recognize elements of your operation here, take heart. You are not doomed to suffer forever the blackguard bricks and mortar that have evolved from noble ideals and humble beginnings. Others have traveled before you and have found a way out of departmental darkness. They have found escape from the maze and mire of manufacturing muda.

The various diseases that manifest themselves in waste have been identified. The vaccination, and if needed, the cure, has been found. The responsibility of each business unit manager is to look past the symptoms, identify the disease, and then apply the correct cure or vaccine in the right amount to their individual organizations.

When you go to the doctor's office, what is the first thing they do? They take your temperature. This provides them a measure against perfection, which to the doctor is somewhere around 98.6° F (37° C). If you are to find out what malady is causing the problem in the business enterprise, you too must first take some measurements. A second reason to perform this step is to provide a benchmark for the future. It is difficult to determine how far you have traveled if you do not know where you started. Therefore, the following exercise is suggested to help you begin the process of describing your current condition.

The mental and visual tool I suggest you think about is a wagon. Think of the wagon you may have pulled as a child. It had four wheels and a handle. A very simple device and mental model. Think about the wagon as representing your business. What do you carry on it? Customers, stakeholders, yourself, your employees, and to a degree, the community in which your company is located. You want it to be a nice smooth ride for everybody, especially your customers. If it is a very bumpy ride, they may find someone else's wagon.

The Lean Enterprise Vehicle

At the end of Chapter One, I invited you to imagine a wagon, and to think of that wagon as representing your business. Figure 2-1 illustrates an ideal wagon, with perfectly concentric wheels of all the same height and size. As you can see, the wheels have a different number of spokes, for reasons to be discussed later. Each wheel is of a size and shape that will ensure as smooth a ride as possible. These wheels are meant to help visualize a measurement tool known as a *radar chart*. The use and interpretation of radar charts will be described shortly.

What is missing? Something to steer with: a handle. If the wagon represents your business, the handle would be the vision of the company. A *company vision* is a guiding set of values and principles that are used to test every decision. It should be clearly communicated and visualized by every member of the team.

Figure 2-1. The ideal Lean enterprise vehicle, with perfectly concentric wheels of the same height and size.

WHEELS, SPOKES, AND THE RADAR CHART

Each *wheel* on the wagon symbolizes one of four critical business principles as plotted on a radar chart. They are:

1. Sales, Production, and Inventory Management,
2. Total Organizational Buy-in,
3. Total Quality Management, and
4. Lean Manufacturing Techniques.

Each wheel, or principle, has a different number of *spokes*, or key indicators. To show more detail about each spoke or key indicator, a radar chart is used. This graphically shows the measurement of each indicator compared against 10, the goal of perfection. The resulting radar chart allows you to visually communicate where the team or company is in relation to defined goals for Total Quality Management (TQM), as shown in Figure 2-2.

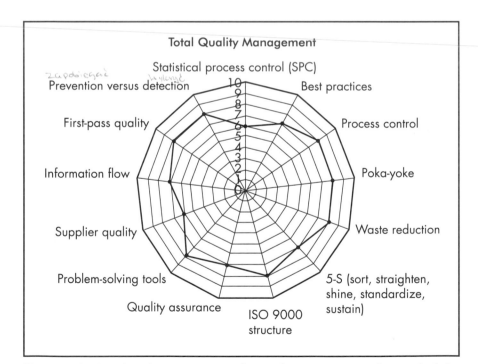

Figure 2-2. A radar chart measuring key indicators against the goal of the perfect 10.

Please note: a perfect 10 is scored against a goal you set for yourself. The goal may change over time as you make improvements. Each company must determine what the goal of 10 means. For example, perfect setup times might be less than 10 minutes long.

The center of the wheel is zero, or the worst score. The outermost area of the wheel is 10, or as close as possible to the goal you have set for yourself. You might use percentages to determine where each indicator is within your company. For example, if your total productive maintenance program is only 60 percent implemented, you might score this indicator six points out of 10.

Each organization must determine which key indicators will tell the most about where it is in the pursuit of perfection. Some indicators may be of the greatest importance to one company and of little consequence to another.

The figures in this chapter illustrate many of the possible spokes or indicators found to be useful. The number of indicators is not meant to overwhelm, but simply to demonstrate the variety of tools at our disposal. Select those indicators which can hold the greatest potential for improvement within your organization first.

Remember that to apply an inordinate amount of attention to one spoke at the neglect of another can result in an inordinately high point and an opposing low point on the wheel (see Figure 2-3). From your customer's perspective, this would create a very rough ride.

Figure 2-3. A not-so-Lean vehicle.

Worse yet, imagine the result of focusing all the improvement efforts of the organization on one or two of the four key business principles, to the total neglect of one or two of the others. It wouldn't take long for the customer to find someone else to ride with if your wagon looked like Figure 2-4!

Figure 2-4. Another not-so-Lean vehicle.

It is better to monitor and manage the improvement of all the key business principles (wheels) and key indicators (spokes) as a whole rather than to focus solely on one or two. Avoid "shotgunning" the ones that make you feel good and ignoring or giving lip service to the others.

In Figure 2-5, you see that all the wheels and spokes are smaller, but they are uniform and should provide a smooth ride, even if the progress will be a bit slower than it would be with full-sized wheels.

Later, I will describe the need to avoid going a "mile wide and an inch deep." This thought and the previous sentence are not at odds. The effective application of a "model line" can and will satisfy the needs of both. A hybrid approach will allow you to give adequate attention to each wheel and spoke and not have your

Figure 2-5. A third not-so-Lean vehicle, but at least this one has uniform-size wheels.

efforts diluted over such a large area. Without a hybrid approach, you risk the system becoming a transparent and brittle veneer.

So, what are the proper measurements? What goals should you set, and how are you to determine where you currently are in relationship to those goals? Let's spend a few moments familiarizing ourselves with each of the wheels on the business wagon. More detail will be added later.

Sales, Production, and Inventory Management

First, take a look at the wheel called Sales, Production, and Inventory Management. There may be one or more spokes that you feel are not important to focus on at the present time. Each company needs to make those decisions for itself. It will be noted strongly when a particular spoke must be measured at every stage of Lean implementation.

People trained in the application of the APICS: The Education Society for Resource Management approach, or those who use Materials Requirement Planning (MRP), Enterprise Requirement Planning (ERP), or other planning tools, will notice that these tools are not identified within this wheel or set of spokes. You may feel compelled to add these to your measurement system.

But first, a disclaimer: comments throughout this text at first may seem to be negative toward the previously mentioned tools, but please reserve judgement. For purchasing, macro-planning, and long-term capacity planning, nothing can beat these tools and techniques. But beware of the notions that setup times are unchangeable, or lead times are fixed between operations and must be considered a given, or that work centers must each have a pile of inventory queued ahead. MRP systems work just fine where they can define and look at a cellular operation as a single machine, disregarding the batch and queue between each step.

Some of the other techniques and tools described in this book can reduce the amount of computer time, paperwork, keystrokes, and non-value-added activities that generate the typical reams of paperwork in the form of work orders, reports, and schedules.

Visual systems, such as *Kanbans* (signals to manufacture or move product), can do much to eliminate the need for complex materials management systems.

This book will not define the finer details and variations of each indicator. Figure 2-6 graphically shows the measurement of each indicator (or spoke of the wheel) compared to 10, the goal of perfection. The resulting radar chart (or wheel) allows you to visually compare the team or company to the defined goals for Sales, Production, and Inventory Management.

Total Organizational Buy-in

The next wheel is shown in Figure 2-7. I refer to this business principle as Total Organizational Buy-in. It relates to the culture within the company. Regardless of how well the rest of the Lean enterprise techniques are applied, the goal of perfection will not be reached if your most important resource, people, is not managed as well as you manage all the other resources.

Total Quality Management

The third wheel, shown earlier in Figure 2-2, illustrates the principle of Total Quality Management (TQM). Books on TQM abound and provide descriptions of all the aspects and benefits of a sound quality program. Whether you choose to use the ISO 9000

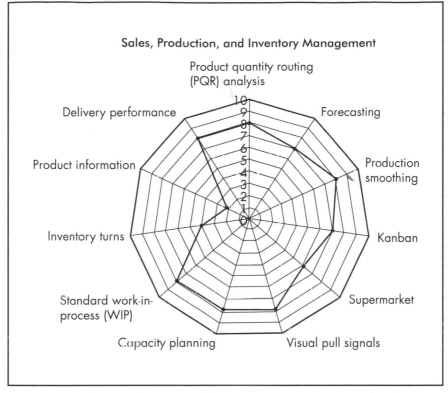

Figure 2-6. Sales, Production, and Inventory Management radar chart.

structure, the Six Sigma approach, the Malcolm Baldridge methodology, or any other quality system, there is truth in the statement that "doing it right the first time" has to be a critical part of the Lean enterprise. Whether we are talking about order entry, engineering, fabrication, assembly, or packaging, the systems must be sound, the practices defined, and the processes capable.

Lean Manufacturing Techniques

The last wheel, and the one we will spend the majority of time discussing in this book, is Lean Manufacturing Techniques, shown in Figure 2-8. There are many tools in the just-in-time tool-box, and the ability to identify the right tool at the right time is what being a Lean mechanic is all about.

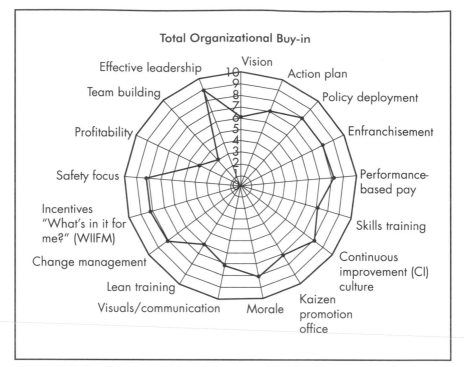

Figure 2-7. Total Organizational Buy-in radar chart, measuring factors affecting the people within the organization.

At one company, we broke down these tools to a list of ten (the team referred to them as their Ten Commandments). They hung an oversized poster over their work cell. Whenever their team was struggling to get past a problem, or when they had hit a performance plateau, they would take time to select the "commandment" most likely to get them past the issue at hand. I could tell you what their "Ten Commandments" were, but it would not be the same list your team might need. One company's list or solution will not fit all companies, much less all the teams that might read this book.

I realize that as you study Figure 2-8, there may be words, phrases, and acronyms that may be foreign to you. Fear not! We will discuss them in detail as we take you on a journey to improve Stan and Fran's business. By the way, did I mention the name of their business? It is, of course, named "The Jobbe Shoppe."

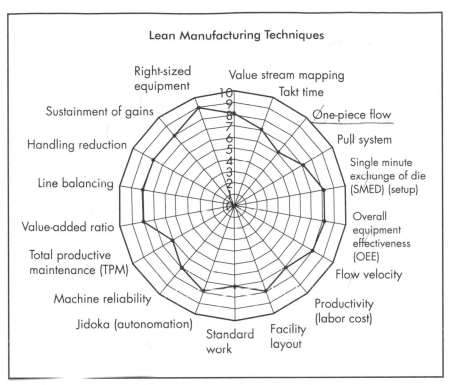

Figure 2-8. Lean Manufacturing Techniques radar chart.

Figure 2-9 shows the complete Lean wagon. All the wheels are shown, and as you can see, they are all uniform and concentric. You also now see the handle of the wagon. In the mental model, the handle symbolizes the company vision, the guiding principles that everyone should be able to see, understand, and use to steer individual decisions. If your company has not developed a vision statement, think about doing it soon. There are many books that can help you get started. I list a few in the bibliography.

Stan and Fran and the rest of The Jobbe Shoppe associates will learn to use the mental model of a wagon and its accompanying wheels (radar charts) to help guide their organization toward full implementation of the Lean enterprise. I invite you to follow along. By way of examples, dialog, and case studies, I will lead you through a potential set of steps for setting up a model line. This is not the only possible approach. But those willing to try these steps should

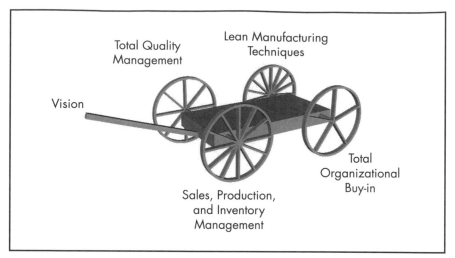

Figure 2-9. The complete Lean wagon.

find them effective. Modification for individual companies is an expectation. Table 2-1 shows the proposed steps in the cellularization of a model line. The list is not in the exact order of the book, but each activity will be discussed.

Table 2-1. Proposed steps to cellularization of a model line

Phase I
1. Perform product-quantity-routing (PQR) data analysis.
2. Identify the product family types.
3. Identify unique value streams.
4. Select a model line.
5. Select a team.
6. Train the team to understand the Lean approach.
7. Develop current condition statement.
8. Develop objective statement.
9. Develop an action plan (Gantt chart time-phased project plan).

Phase II
1. Collect operator cycle times.
2. Collect machine cycle times.
3. Map the value stream.

Table 2-1. (continued)

4. Obtain the best forecast and history information available.
5. Develop Takt time for three production levels.
6. Identify equipment requirements.
7. Identify shared equipment.
8. Re-engineer product flows on paper.

Phase III

1. Develop a future state map (conceptual).
2. Team training (how to operate as a cell).
3. Cross-train the team (use training matrix).
4. Virtually link upstream and downstream processes.
5. Implement the "buddy check" inspection process.
6. Train the team in the Kaizen approach.
7. Perform setup reduction projects.
8. Develop setup reduction charts.
9. Develop first-pass quality process.
10. Develop standard work for three production levels.
11. Educate teams in use of standard work.
12. Balance the line.
13. Apply 5-S (workplace organization: sort, strengthen, shine, standardize, sustain).
14. Insure machine reliability.
15. Begin total productive maintenance (TPM) procedures.
16. Reduce material handling.
17. Implement linearity charts for waste and production.
18. Reduce paperwork.

Phase IV

1. Develop pull signals.
2. Work with vendors to supply raw materials "just-in-time."
3. Implement standard work-in-process (WIP) (or supermarkets).
4. Implement limited finished goods inventory (FGI) to help smooth the order file.
5. Reduce non-value-added activities.
6. Apply Jidoka techniques (autonomation).
7. Test the system (run it!).
8. Document results.
9. Modify, improve.

Table 2-1. (continued)

Phase V
1. Implement performance-based pay.
2. Document new "best practices."
3. Second setup reduction on bottleneck operations.
4. Design and build right-size equipment.
5. Develop detail layout.
6. Execute the move.
7. Identify the next value stream and repeat.

3

Introduction to a Small Manufacturing Company

In Chapter One, we met Fran and Stan. It is now 10 years into the development of their company, The Jobbe Shoppe. They are experiencing growing pains, including a fair amount of difficulty induced from customer reaction to lead time issues and a never-ending demand for cost improvements.

One day, AZTec's buyer informs Fran that he will be out of town for the next week, participating in a Kaizen event. Fran had never heard the word "Kaizen" before, and hesitated to ask, afraid of looking ignorant.

UNDERSTANDING KAIZEN

Fran immediately got out the dictionary to look up the word, but it wasn't there. Maybe she had misheard. She asked Stan, who replied, *"Kaizen* is a Japanese word for making people work smarter." He added, "We already make new improvements every day."

A year later, Stan was invited to participate in a Kaizen event at AZTec. When your customer invites you, you have to go. When Stan asked what he should bring, the reply was, "Just bring your mind, and be prepared for five days and one night." That seemed like a silly thing to say, but Stan discovered again, the customer is always right. Stan's days were long and the nights were short. It was hard for him to sleep. Once into the mode of creative thought, the mind is a fertile ground for improvement ideas, even at night.

It was the beginning of the end of waste at the Jobbe Shoppe. By participating in the Kaizen event, Stan learned that they were not applying Kaizen every day and they were not getting better. In fact, they were surrounded by waste at every turn.

PERFORMANCE EVALUATION

Stan realized that The Jobbe Shoppe needed to re-establish the simplistic nature of the small shop he and Fran had first started. They also needed to regain the relationship of trust and dependability with their customers that existed in the beginning. Stan began to see that the only way The Jobbe Shoppe could return to the level of performance it had 10 years before was to utilize the principles of Lean.

The leadership of AZTec understood how difficult it might be for Stan and his small company to gain the knowledge and skills necessary to implement the Lean approach. Consultants can cost quite a bit, and Stan had no real life examples and models. It might never happen. So the vice-president of operations at AZTec partnered up one of their continuous improvement technicians, Jan, with Stan to begin the process of "Leaning" out The Jobbe Shoppe. Not every customer is as accommodating as AZTec. But the vice-president knew that for AZTec to be truly successful, The Jobbe Shoppe had to be successful as well. AZTec had been working for the last four years to become Lean and now the time was right to begin looking at the vendor base portion of their value stream for improvement.

Stan was a little uneasy about Jan's first visit. Having the customer come into the plant to view all the warts could not be positive for the business. However, Jan put Stan's mind at ease right away by spending a few minutes describing AZTec's experience. Jan also described how they developed a keen sense of awareness for waste, and yet did not use such findings as a reason to discipline or chastise employees or suppliers. Finding waste became a positive rather than negative experience. Discovering and eliminating muda was a reason to celebrate rather than roll on the floor in agony. Jan referred to it as goldmining and every discovery was a reason to applaud the efforts of the team and the company.

Value Stream Mapping^{SM}

"So, where do we start?" Stan asked. Jan explained that the first thing to do is to make a record of their current activities so that next month, next year, or five years down the road, Stan could look back and see if there had been progress. Value Stream

Mapping^{SM} can help illustrate improvements and progress made. "So do you want me to have our engineer draw a material flow diagram?" Stan asked.

"Not exactly, Stan," Jan answered "Let me show you an example of a value stream map." Jan pulled out a piece of paper with a sketch. It described a fictitious manufacturing process (see Figure 3-1).

Jan went on to explain what each symbol meant and how the map showed the inventory, material handling, and flow of material and information.

"You see, Stan, there may be five, 10, or 25 distinct value streams for different products in your plant right now. A value stream map is a tool to help sort all the product types into distinct families. It assists you in visualizing, identifying, and eliminating all forms of waste. We generally begin by selecting one of these product groups to use as a "model line." The first step after selecting a model line is to "map" the entire manufacturing process for this product family.

"By applying all the Lean manufacturing techniques to this model, you can develop a positive in-house example of how the entire plant should operate. For instance, you can take future value stream teams on a tour of the model line to show them how fast setup programs are developed, or how 5-S (sort, straighten, shine, standardize, and sustain) can help them get organized, or how pull systems and kanbans work."

"How do we choose which value stream or product family to map?" Stan asked.

"Good question. There are many ways to select a value stream. You might select a product type such as panels or card cages. You could select a particular size of product, such as parts that are smaller than a breadbox. Or, your choice could be customer-specific. You might find it best to select a model line based on material-specific requirements. For example, aluminum or stainless steel products might be separated into distinct value streams since the process steps might be vastly different."

Product-Quantity-Routing Analysis

Jan continued, "A common tool used by companies to help them perform this selection process is a technique called the *PQR*

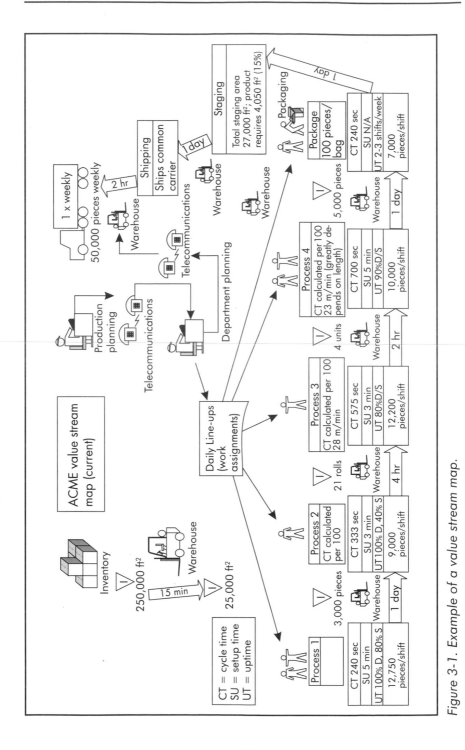

Figure 3-1. Example of a value stream map.

analysis. *PQR* stands for 'Product Quantity Routing,' which is a short way of saying what is it that we make, how much, and what machines we use to make it."

"Uh-oh, this is starting to sound complicated," Stan worried out loud.

"Not at all," Jan reassured him. "We'll let the computer do the work for us." Jan reached into his briefcase and retrieved a file folder. "For example, look at this spreadsheet. The top portion shows a listing of some part numbers and the processes that they go through. It's kind of hard to see any patterns here, but if you sort the part numbers by common processes in a spreadsheet you begin to see a pattern develop. In the bottom portion of the spreadsheet, the same list is sorted. Can you see which part numbers have similar process requirements?"

"Yes. It's obvious that part numbers X-1C and Y-10 should probably be a part of the same family group, and so should X-20 and Z-5," Stan answered. "But what if part numbers X, Y, and Z are all sold to different customers?"

Jan returned the question. "I would ask you, is it more important to keep parts together, even if they are dissimilar, just because they will ultimately be sold to the same customer, or is it more reasonable to group parts together that require similar equipment or processes?"

"Well, if it were possible to coordinate all the parts to finish at the right time, the customer wouldn't care where in the shop they were made," Stan guessed.

"I believe you are right. With that in mind, I'd say that most companies working to develop a model line will perform a search to find the products most alike in process so that they can group machines together that will not be either under- or over-utilized. Later, we will discuss standard work and how it becomes critical that work content not vary a great deal from part to part. Selecting parts that require similar processes will avoid such problems," Jan explained.

Stan, anxious to get started, asked, "How do we select our model line?"

"We need a list of all your part numbers, the quantity ordered over the last year, and all the process steps they go through. Do you have access to this information for the last 12 months?"

Stan puzzled for a moment. "I think we can run a report that will tell us everything produced in the last year but it won't necessarily identify each process step. Is that important?"

"It would be helpful, but we can fill that in ourselves with a planner or manufacturing lead-person in the room," Jan reassured him. "How long will it take your computer team to run a report?"

"We can have it before we get back from lunch. Are you hungry yet?" Stan walked Jan to the planning office.

What Stan and Jan will develop is a larger version of the PQR spreadsheet shown in Table 3-1. They will use it to begin sorting out the various product families and value streams. This spreadsheet can be expanded to include all the potential part numbers

Table 3-1. Example of product-quantity-routing spreadsheet

		Unsorted			
			Processes		
Product Name	Production Volume	Shear	Press	Bend	Weld
X-1	1,000	1	2	3	4
X-1C	1,500	1		2	3
X-20	1,800		1	2	3
X 20B	900		1		2
Y-10	700	1		2	3
Z-5	200		1	2	3

		Sorted			
			Processes		
Product Name	Production Volume	Shear	Press	Bend	Weld
X-1C	1,500	1		2	3
Y-10	700	1		2	3
X-20	1,800		1	2	3
Z-5	200		1	2	3
X 20B	900		1		2
X-1	1,000	1	2	3	4

and work steps. At this point the spreadsheet does not include warehouse or non-value-added steps. We will deal with this later when we begin mapping the value stream. In this step, identify only the part number and its value-added manufacturing requirements. Table 3-2 illustrates how this tool is used.

As an alternative to using a computer, write down all the same information on small recipe cards, along with the required process steps for each product, and then group the like cards together into product families.

By identifying the part number and the processes involved, you can use PQR analysis to begin sorting out similarities among processes and individual parts. It is helpful to number the steps in case there is backtracking or backflow in the current process. Alternatively, you can insert a column for the same process more than once, as shown in Table 3-2 with the drill. This avoids some sorting problems caused by backflow or multiple steps through the same process.

It is difficult to identify a pattern looking at Table 3-3. Besides the fact that everything gets sheared, other similarities between parts are harder to see. By using the power of the computer, we can sort according to similar processes.

It is not unusual for a job shop to have 3,000 or more part numbers. You can see that performing this necessary task by hand could be a bit time consuming. If you have a computer database, you might use this tool to speed up the process. Writing a query or report for this information can save enormous amounts of time. Table 3-4 shows a sorted version of the same data. Notice how much easier it is to identify the groups of parts that should likely be part of the same value stream.

Suppose Stan and Jan decide to use the eight part numbers grouped at the top of this list as a model for developing a value stream map. Since the part numbers all weld, hardware, and form, this may be a good candidate. When performing the PQR analysis, you want to look for the common denominator.

Another reason to use the PQR is to assist teams in locating the "low hanging fruit" (easy to gain improvements). Be careful to select projects that are meaningful to the future of the company. You do not want to set up a model line in an area or for a product type that will be run infrequently or for a project that has run its course and will soon be phased out.

Table 3-2. Example of product routing worksheet

Part Number	Shear	Stamp	Punch	Laser	Drill	Deburr	Laser	Drill	Form	Hardware	Tap	Weld	Annual Demand	Monthly Demand
100706	1		2			3			4				613	51
100706	1	2							3	4		5	504	42
100898	1	2							3	4		5	175	15
100233	1		2			3			4				923	77

Table 3-3. Unsorted product-quantity-routing worksheet

Part Number	Shear	Stamp	Punch	Laser	Drill	Deburr	Laser	Drill	Form	Hardware	Tap	Weld	Annual	Monthly
100706	1		2			3			4				613	51
100706	1	2							3	4		5	504	42
100898	1	2							3	4		5	175	15
100233	1		2			3			4				923	77
100233	1			2				3				4	375	31
100233	1				2		3				4		184	15
100233	1		2			3	4						615	51
100233	1				2	3		4					365	30
100233	1		2				3		4			5	1,240	103
100233	1		2			3			4				1,020	85
100233	1		2						3		4		2,542	212
100233	1		2			3			4				63,413	5,284
100233	1	2							3	4		5	75,013	6,251
100233	1	2							3			4	1,770	148
100233	1			2				3		4			307	26
100233	1									4		4	942	79
100234	1	2							3		4		608	51

35

Table 3-3. (continued)

Part Number	Shear	Stamp	Punch	Laser	Drill	Deburr	Laser	Drill	Form	Hardware	Tap	Weld	Annual	Monthly
100234	1			2				3					119	10
100234	1		2			3			4				16,587	1,382
100234	1	2							3	4		5	19,112	1,593
100356	1		2						3				30,811	2,568
100356	1			2			3						1,451	121
100356	1			2			3						196	16
100358	1		2						3				10,354	863
100413	1			2			3						287	24
100413	1		2						3				25,116	2,093
100413	1			2				3					693	58
100497	1		2			3			4			5	175	15
100497	1	2							3	4			367	31

Table 3-4. Sorted product-quantity-routing worksheet

Part Number	Shear	Stamp	Punch	Laser	Drill	Deburr	Laser	Drill	Form	Hardware	Tap	Weld	Annual	Monthly
100706	1	2							3	4		5	504	42
100898	1	2							3	4		5	175	15
100233	1	2							3	4		5	75,013	6,251
100233	1	2							3			4	1,770	148
100233	1	2							3			4	307	26
100234	1	2							3	4		5	19,112	1,593
100497	1	2							3	4		5	367	31
100233	1	2					3			4		5	1,240	103
100706	1		2			3			4				613	51
100233	1		2			3			4				923	77
100233	1		2			3			4				1,020	85
100233	1		2			3			4				63,413	5,284
100234	1		2			3			4				16,587	1,382
100497	1		2			3			4				175	15
100233	1		2						3		4		2,542	212
100234	1		2						3		4		608	51
100356	1		2						3				30,811	2,568
100358	1		2						3				10,354	863

Table 3-4. (continued)

Part Number	Shear	Stamp	Punch	Laser	Drill	Deburr	Laser	Drill	Form	Hardware	Tap	Weld	Annual	Monthly
100413	1		2						3				25,116	2,093
100233	1		2			3	4						615	51
100356	1			2			3						1,451	121
100356	1			2			3						196	16
100413	1			2			3						287	24
100233	1			2				3				4	375	31
100233	1			2				3		4		4	942	79
100234	1			2				3					119	10
100413	1			2				3					693	58
100233	1				2		3				4		184	15
100233	1				2	3		4					365	30

You can sort and visually show the same data using a Pareto diagram, thus allowing you to see what products you make the most. This is a good place to start. The 80/20 rule can help you select a meaningful portion of your ongoing order file to use as a model line. The selection criteria for a model line should include a measurement regarding the moderate and stable nature of the ordering patterns, both quantity and regularity.

Figure 3-2 shows a Pareto graph representing the quantity (by part number) for the data. The bars shown on the left side of the chart are the tallest and show the greatest number of parts produced on an annual basis. These part numbers may be good candidates for use as a model line if they use similar manufacturing processes.

By using PRQ analysis and a Pareto diagram, you can narrow down the best candidate for a model line. Then, map the entire value stream of the product family chosen as a model line.

What is a *value stream map*? It is a visual tool to assist you in identifying and eliminating all forms of waste. For example, it is quite likely that between the shear and the stamping operation, Stan and Jan will find material being moved with a forklift, possibly being stored in a rack or warehouse. The material would no doubt be ticketed for identification, logged onto the computer, and when required at the stamping press, moved again, counted again, inspected for damage incurred while being moved stored, and so forth. All these activities take time but add no value from the perspective of the customer. We want to identify all the steps needed and all the time involved in the process for this type of part.

Why don't we just go out and tell the operators to work faster, harder, and smarter? Then we wouldn't have to deal with the effort of developing the PQR analysis and value stream map. The fundamental reason we are trying to become Lean is to lower costs and decrease lead time. It can be defined in this simple equation: lead time = increased cost.

Value-added versus Non-value-added Activities

The typical approach taken in the past has been to focus on the manufacturing processes, the value-added process steps. Very often, little attention is given to the non-value-added activities such

39

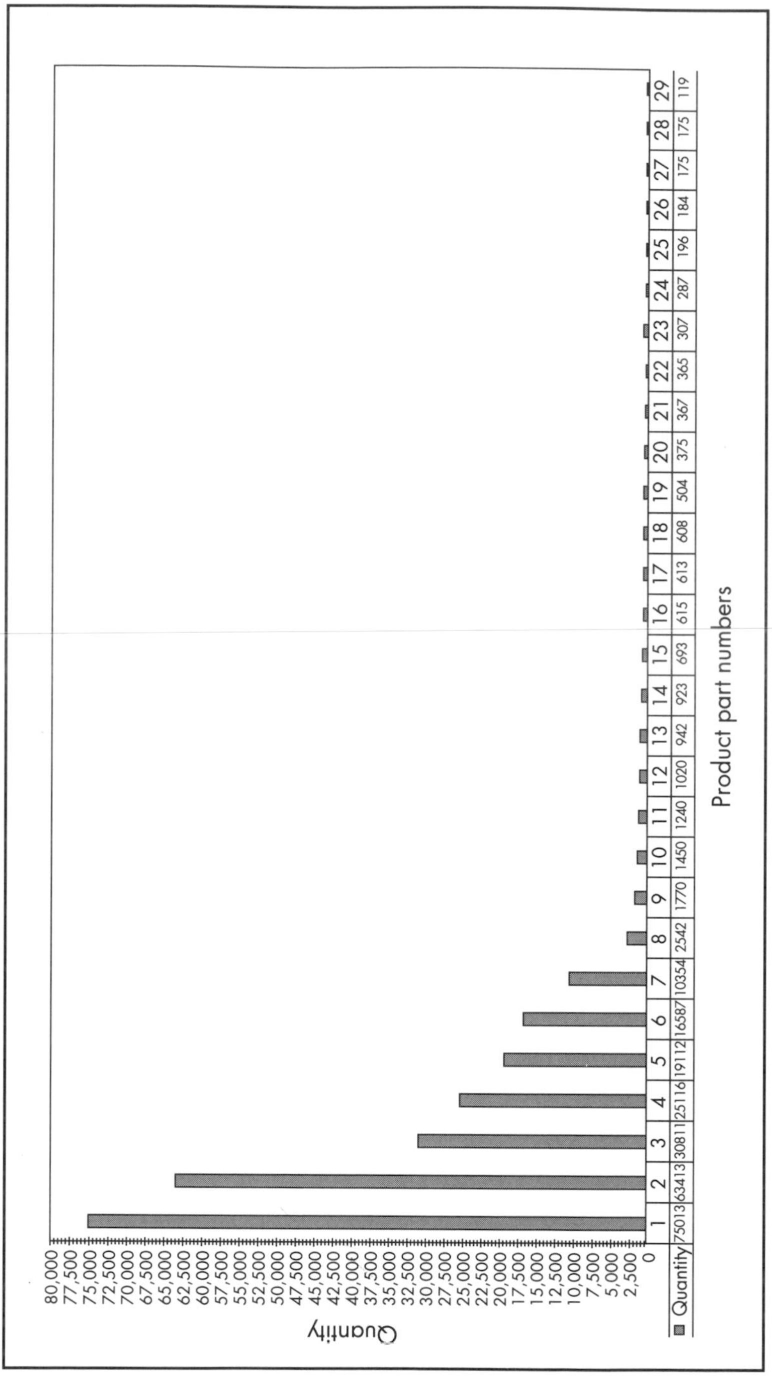

Quantity	1	2	3	4	5	6	7	8	9	10	11	12	13	14	15	16	17	18	19	20	21	22	23	24	25	26	27	28	29
Quantity	75013	63413	30811	25116	19112	16587	10354	2542	1770	1450	1240	1020	942	923	693	615	613	608	504	375	367	365	307	287	196	184	175	175	119

Product part numbers

Figure 3-2. Pareto chart showing product quantity data.

40

as storage and transportation. The result is that minimal effect is realized on overall lead time. For example, studies indicate that when you examine lead time, you will find something similar to Figure 3-3. The two percentages equal total lead time.

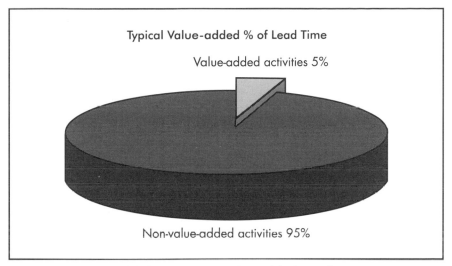

Figure 3-3. Value-added versus non-value-added pie chart.

If you spend all your energies trying to improve the value-added component of lead time, and even if you were able to cut that time in half, the improvement to lead time would be only 2.5 percent. It reminds me of an old joke about a bum searching under the streetlight for a cigar butt that he dropped. When a passerby stops to ask if he is all right, the bum remains stooped over as he describes his problem. The passerby asks where he thinks he dropped it. Without looking up, the bum answers, "Across the street." Shocked, the passerby asks, "Well then, why aren't you looking over there?" The bum straightens up and says, "The light is better over here!"

We often look for opportunity in the value-added component while overlooking an easier solution to lead time reduction. A better approach might be to do everything you possibly can to improve the value-added component, but focus first on the non-value-added component of lead time. If you cut the non-value-added time in half, your lead time improvement would look like the chart in Figure 3-4. Nearly a 50 percent reduction in lead time. Quite a difference!

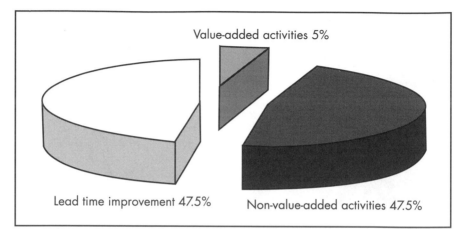

Value-added activities 5%

Lead time improvement 47.5%   Non-value-added activities 47.5%

Figure 3-4. Potential effect on lead time after reducing non-value-added activities by 50 percent.

Waste

Material based on the Toyota Production System lists seven major forms of waste:

1. Waste from overproduction,
2. Waste from waiting,
3. Transportation waste,
4. Processing waste,
5. Inventory waste,
6. Waste of motion, and
7. Waste from product defects.

To make many forms of waste visible, the value stream map process works best if you map not only the material flow, but also the information flow, the inventory (WIP) storage, and the flow process. Also included would be transportation flow, non-value-added activities required in the current process, and the material flow through the value-added steps.

ABCs of Waste Reduction

Finding waste is as easy as ABC: activities, behaviors, and conditions. As you map the value streams, ask questions at each step of the process, using ABC as a mental checklist:

1. What activities are happening here? Do the activities add value or waste time?
2. What behaviors are demonstrated, Lean or wasteful?
3. Do conditions foster an environment of urgency or do they permit waste?

Here is a partial list of activities, behaviors, and conditions that can lead to waste:

- Facility layout,
- Excessive setup times,
- Incapable process (discussed in a later chapter),
- Poor preventive maintenance,
- Uncontrolled work method,
- Lack of training,
- Lack of workplace organization,
- Lack of supplier quality and reliability,
- Lack of concern (accountability),
- Passing on defective parts,
- Not communicating improvements, and
- Redundant counting or ticketing.

The purpose of the value stream map is to help identify as many of these waste opportunities as possible. It may be helpful to carry this list with you as you travel the value stream.

Value Stream Mapping^{SM} is a Service Mark of the Lean Enterprise Institute.

4

Value Stream Mapping^SM

Stan and Jan are about to begin mapping the value stream they have chosen. Before they begin, Jan goes through a question exercise with Stan.

"Stan, whenever I am explaining a new process to someone, I try to answer six questions: what, why, who, when, where, and how. So, the first question, 'what?'. What is the value stream map? It is a visual tool for identifying all activities in the planning and manufacturing process. We map out these steps to make both value-added and non-value-added activities easy to recognize.

"For 'why?', you ask this: why go to the trouble of documenting a process that we know we are going to change? It is necessary to document the current condition so we can visualize what might otherwise go unnoticed. Non-value-added activities and issues that add to lead-time are usually invisible within the process.

"Now let's talk about 'who?', and that means, who needs to be involved? The people who are the primary leaders of the product family we have selected. The product family leaders, or value stream leaders, will ultimately be the ones charged with implementation, so they need to understand the conditions that exist now. We call this the *current state map*. We will develop another map to show how the process should look. We refer to this as the *future state map*.

"The question 'when?' is a tricky one. In what order should the mapping process be done? There is a tendency to skip over the current map and go right to the future state map. But if we don't know the current process, we can't really make intelligent decisions about how the future state should look.

"The question 'where?' is important. Where should the value stream map be developed? I recommend that the work be done on the shop floor. You cannot effectively do this at a desk a hundred feet from the shop floor. Opinions and estimates will never be accurate enough to make the kinds of decisions the team will need to make. We have to encourage the Value Stream Mapping[SM] team to go out onto the floor and look for themselves.

VALUE STREAM SYMBOLS

"The last question, 'how?', is a little more involved. I've brought along some training material from our own in-house efforts. I think that these five pages break down the process into manageable and understandable steps. The first page shows some of the symbols we will use to develop our value stream maps. We may not use all the symbols, but together I can show you what each of them means."

Figure 4-1 shows some value stream symbols. These sample symbols are not meant to represent the only symbols you can use. Some people use forklifts, tables or carts to show how material is moved. These are meant to be examples only. The "process" symbol is used to describe each step of manufacturing or assembly. A symbol for "vendor" allows you to capture data related to outside work. A "data box" offers you a place to record information about cycle times (CT), changeover times (CO), how many shifts are available, and whether there is a built in scrap rate (that is, saw kerf). The triangle-shaped symbol is used to show how much inventory is stored at each work-in-process (WIP) location. Arrows of any shape or color can be used to signify how material is moved or from where it is obtained. The "supermarket" symbol can show storage locations of standard WIP (pre-determined stock or Kanban). A curved arrow can be used to show a physical move or consumption from a Kanban or supermarket location. Finally, the little figure of the truck in Figure 4-2 allows you to make the shipment amounts or frequency visible to anyone reading the value stream map. Figure 4-2 shows delivery and sales demand icons and Figure 4-3 shows Value Stream Mapping icons.

"Actually, this doesn't look too complicated. When can we start?" Stan anxiously asks. "Are there any books or training materials that I can use to get our teams up to speed with Value Stream Mapping?"

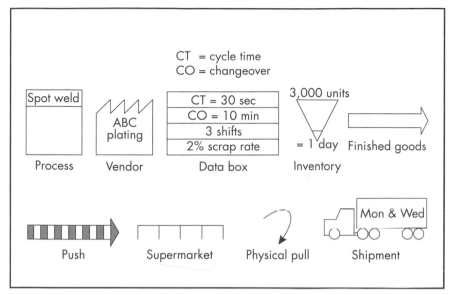

Figure 4-1. Value stream map symbols.

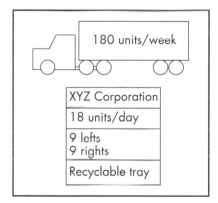

Figure 4-2. Delivery and sales demand icons.

Jan can't help but smile at Stan's enthusiasm. "First question first. We can start tomorrow morning, if you wish. The nice thing about this is that the shop does not have to be running the exact material you are mapping at the moment you perform the Value Stream Mapping process. We can get a lot done by talking face-to-face with the operators."

"Okay. Thanks. I'll pull our team together in the morning. I will also have an engineer and a computer available so we can have him draw the maps." Stan begins gathering up all the paperwork on the table.

"Well, let's talk about that," Jan interrupts. "Take a look at the last item listed under Step 1. Do you notice it recommends using a pencil rather than a computer? Can you guess why they recommend that?"

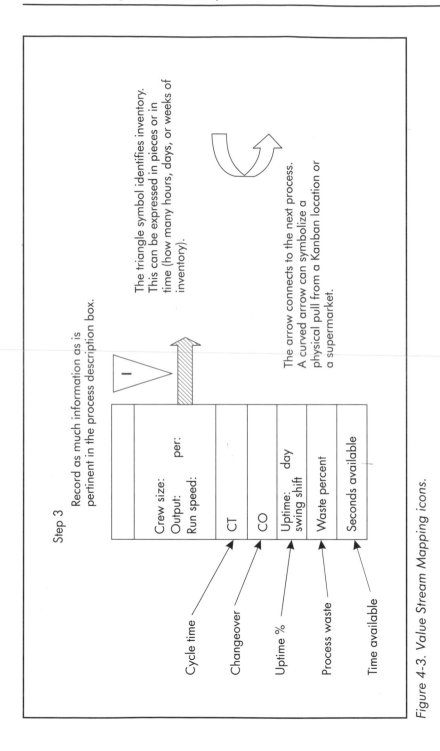

Figure 4-3. Value Stream Mapping icons.

"I guess it might be that a computer is hard to move through the shop?"

"That's part of it. In addition to the logistics of using a computer in the shop, the average employee may not have the computer skills that you and I have. Since this is a tool for them, we don't want to have someone else, an engineer for example, do the work for them. This would have the effect of minimizing their participation and thus create less ownership in the process."

"That makes sense. Okay, what should I have ready for morning?"

"Just the coffee," Jan jokes. "And some blank paper, pencils, a tape measure, a stop watch, and a calculator. If we plan to spend an hour or so with the team doing some basic training and going over these five sheets, I think we will be ready to go."

"We'll be ready. If I can keep these, I'll make copies for everybody. See you in the morning. Is 8:00 a.m. okay with you?"

"Works great for me. See you then." Jan shakes Stan's hand as they part company.

FOUR STEPS TO VALUE STREAM MAPPING

The process of documenting all activities in value-stream mapping occurs in four steps: product development, process design, preparation, and planning.

Step 1: Product Development

- Identify customer requirements,
- Define method of delivery, and
- Define typical quantity requirements.

This value stream can serve more than one customer, but be sure to use similar primary processes. Use a pencil rather than a computer.

Step 2: Process Design

Perform an upstream walk-through for each process step, observing and documenting as much of the following as possible:

- Cycle time (operator and machine cycle time),
- Changeover times,

- Average inventory queue,
- Average production batch size,
- Number of operators at each process,
- Package or container size,
- Available time (take out break and lunch times),
- Scrap rate,
- Machine up-time (availability), and
- Number of product variations.

Step 3: Preparation

Record as much information as is pertinent in the process description box.

Step 4: Planning

- Develop a future state map,
- Dream about perfection (imagineering),
- Think outside the box,
- Develop alternatives to the current state map that are muda-free, and
- Focus on velocity.

Test each idea against TOP. That is, does it support Takt time, one-piece flow, and pull? (This will be explained later.)

- Break down the future state map into manageable steps,
- Develop a Gantt chart (time-phased project plan), and
- Identify the Kaikaku and Kaizen events that will need to take place.

Figure 4-4 (computer-generated for clarity) shows a blank value stream map with areas available to identify all the material flow diagram components. Figure 4-5 shows what a completed map might look like after Stan and Jan finish it.

The process defined in Figure 4-5 shows the current value stream map for the material that Stan and his team have selected for the model line. Notice the box in the lower right corner. This area and the information given are used to calculate the value-added ratio. This is a very important measurement, and will be explained in the next chapter.

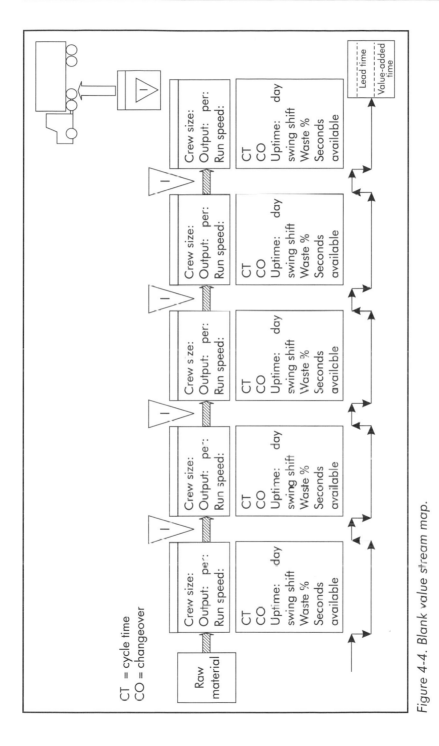

Figure 4-4. Blank value stream map.

51

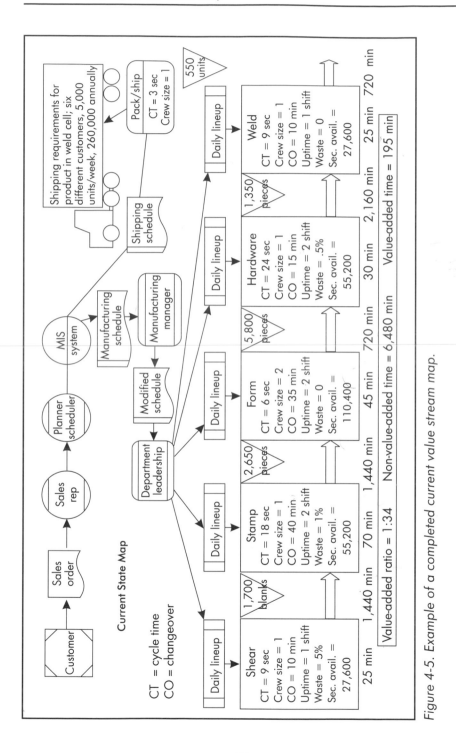

Figure 4-5. Example of a completed current value stream map.

Figure 4-6 shows Stan and Jan's plan for the future. This is a conceptual rather than a detailed layout. We will refer back to this figure many times in this book.

Notice that in the future state map the information driving this process flows toward the customer, rather than away from the customer as shown in the current state map (Figure 4-5). This improvement will be possible if the goal of implementing a Just-in-Time delivery system is fully realized. This may take time to implement, but remember, this is a future state map, an ideal situation. It may take months or even years to complete, but giving the team a clear and defined goal will help them focus on the future.

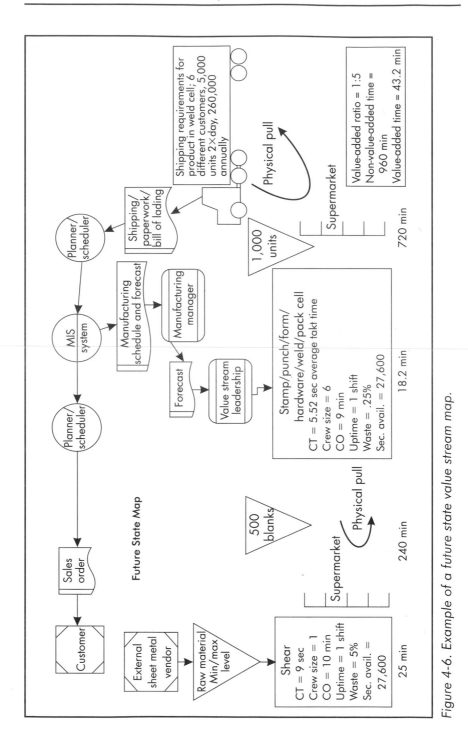

Figure 4-6. Example of a future state value stream map.

Lead Time and Activity

Once Stan and Jan complete the value stream maps, they can use them to calculate the value-added ratio of the current process and to set goals for the future. These are powerful tools to define and make visible the gap between lead time and value-added activity.

Here is how it works. Let's use an example of a sheet metal process. As a part of the mapping process, Stan and Jan go to the shop and measure all the processing time for a random part number, as shown in Table 5-1. This is not waste-free time, but it is the actual operator time taken to process 100 parts through each operation.

If you look only at the value-added steps, 120 minutes or two hours of processing time does not really sound so bad. However, due to the number of other projects ahead of it, this job of only 100 parts takes five days to weave its way through the shop. In fact, the customer will have to wait five and a half days, or 7,920 minutes, for his parts. This gap is the value-added ratio.

Table 5-1. Value-added versus nonvalue-added time

	Operational Time		Lead Time
Shear	10 blanks	= 15 min	1 day
Stamp	10 blanks	= 30 min	1 day
Form	100 parts	= 10 min	.5 day
Hardware	100 parts	= 40 min	1 day
Weld	100 parts	= 15 min	1.5 days
Pack	100 parts	= 10 min	.5 day
Total		120 min	5.5 days (7,920 min)

DEALING WITH DIFFERENT PROCESSES

This chapter will discuss three necessary considerations when evaluating and improving lead-time and supporting activities:

1. Value-added and non-value added ratios,
2. Product demand patterns, and
3. Process flexibility.

Value-added versus Non-value-added Ratios

One way to express the value-added ratio is to calculate what percentage of the lead-time is value-added and what percentage is non-value-added. In the example shown in Table 5-2, the ratio is 1:33. This means that for each minute a project is worked on, it is sitting for 33 minutes. It is hard to imagine a process where the ratio would ever be 1:1, because there is always some handling. However, this shouldn't stop anyone from trying to improve the system.

Forward-thinking companies seeking to apply the Lean enterprise approach are focusing on a value-added ratio goal of 1:10. This means for each hour the material is being processed, it will be allowed to be resident in the manufacturing process for 10 hours. This is easier said than done. However, it is possible to change the imbalance between value-added and non-value-added activities. These activities manifest themselves as excessive lead times, and in turn, lead to enormous wastes of effort, time, and resources.

Becoming Lean is as simple as identifying where the non-value-added actions are taking place, selecting the right tool to elimi-

Table 5-2. Value-added ratio example

Operator cycle time	195 min
Lead time	6,480 min
Non-value-added time	6,285 min
Value-added, percent	3.01
Non-value-added, percent	96.99
Value-added ratio	1:33

nate the non-value-added actions, and then not allowing the repair to come undone. Then, doing it again and again, every day.

No two companies or even two teams are the same. Depending on size, number of customers, sales distribution (mix), and a multitude of other factors, there are endless differences and therefore numerous approaches to applying the Lean approach to the job shop. A job shop may not need the same tools applied at Toyota or Harley Davidson. A hybrid approach may be necessary.

Product Demand Patterns

Because of the consistent nature of the product flowing through most Original Equipment Manufacturing (OEM) plants or dedicated assembly processes, the application of focused layout, running to Takt time, and pulling one piece at a time is obviously the logical approach. It is ridiculous for anyone in this category to be batching material through departments. On the other hand, a hybrid approach is usually the best option for the number of unique challenges that job shops face. For example, if you are trying to make a job shop more Lean, you will discover by using the Product Quantity Routing (PQR) analysis that the parts you produce may have very distinctive demand patterns, and therefore fall into one of the four categories shown in Figure 5-1. Very few job shops ever see many part numbers falling into the category identified "smooth." This reality has led to the conclusion that if you can determine the approximate percentage of your parts that fall into each of these categories, then it makes sense to divide the shop into two or more hybrid systems. The systems then can be set up to deal specifically with the differences.

In one case, owners of a medium-sized shop ($20 million annual sales) realized that their sales volume could be divided into three unique demand pattern types. So they divided their shop into three distinct departments (see Table 5-3).

Your operation will have unique customer demands, special process requirements, or limitations created by shared resources that will determine different percentages from those shown here. You can be very good at the "core" business while retaining the nimble and flexible nature of a job shop.

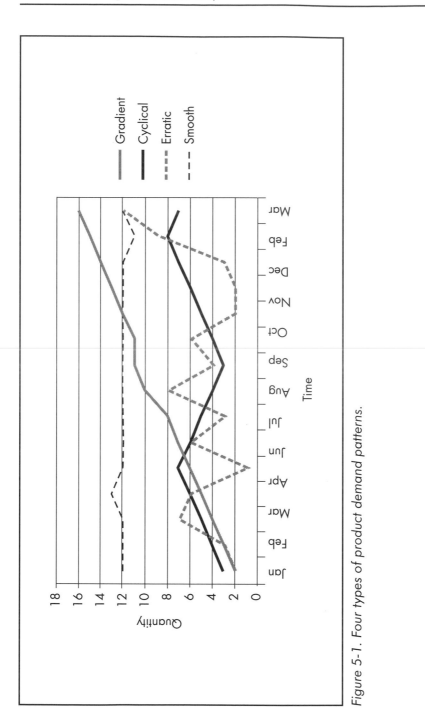

Figure 5-1. Four types of product demand patterns.

Table 5-3. Hybrid approach to Lean manufacturing in a job shop

Special Cells 15% Sales	Standard Cells 25% Sales	Just-in-Time (JIT) Cells 60% Sales
Prototypes	Proven CNC programs	All the conditions of the standard cell apply plus:
Untested CNC programs	Parts that will run again	Customer forecasts fairly accurate
One-of-a-kind special tooling	Setups documented	Customers buy into JIT programs
Engineered to order	Quality needs are defined	Vendors support the required lead times

Process Flexibility

Many companies, especially job shops, miss the mark because they believe, or they are told, that they have an "either-or" decision. A hybrid approach would allow the shop to do both very well, instead of one or the other miserably.

Some companies design their entire manufacturing process around the "just in case" scenario. They should follow the 80/20 rule, setting up their shop to effectively flow the products that make up 80 percent of what they produce. Instead, they set up their machinery to effectively deal with the exceptional part numbers ("dogs and cats") that give them fits and jerks. Now, they have a plant where not only the "problem-child" parts are a problem, but even the 80 percent "bread-and-butter" parts become a problem.

It is easy to get caught trying to be all things to all people. That's the reason very few machine tool manufacturers design "right-sized equipment" (small equipment designed for quick setup and often dedicated to a small number of parts). Their customers have historically wanted huge one-size-fits-all machines that can pump out parts by the hundreds or thousands per hour. The trouble with this approach is that the setup times usually become inordinately long. The equipment becomes so complex that it takes a mechanical engineer to use it, maintain it, or set it up. The same is true of a one-size-fits-all manufacturing system. Being Lean requires management to think holistically rather than focusing on the output efficiency of one or two machines.

Keep in mind that what you are after is not optimization of one machine, but rather an improvement in productivity, elimination of waste, and an increase in product velocity through the entire plant. This may mean changing the way managers manage. Many leaders have to learn to macro-manage rather than micro-manage. To see the entire productivity picture (rather than sub-optimization of one machine), leaders must stand back far enough to see whether the material is flowing or not. Idle material is worse than an idle machine. It is not good for a machine to produce parts if the next process cannot accept them. This results in more and more material that no one can use.

If you identify and separate the product family types, perform the PQR analysis, and then set up the process to deal most effectively with the 80 percent, the 20 percent will take care of itself. If you insure that you are effectively processing the bread-and-butter parts, you will have plenty of time to deal with the dogs and cats.

Be good at finishing. It is better to do one thing well than 10 things miserably. People may have short memories, but not for management's failures to fulfill commitments. Build some success stories and celebrate the journey.

Let's go back to The Jobbe Shoppe and observe the efforts of Stan, Jan, and the rest of the team as they develop a future state map. They will then begin the process of building a strategic plan of action to improve the value-added ratio of their model line.

Optimum Lot Size

Stan, Jan, and the rest of the team are meeting for the first time since the value stream maps were completed. They have selected the model line, a welding cell. Their next step is to begin the process of developing the model line. Jan has encouraged Stan to spend a day training the team in the fundamentals of the Toyota production system before they start. Jan will handle the training, which includes a simulation exercise that shows the advantage of a one-piece flow system as compared to a batch manufacturing system. A plastic building block set available at any toy store is used (see Figure 6-1). The simulation is a hybrid overview of the Toyota production system.

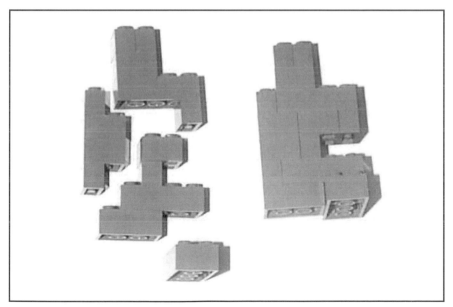

Figure 6-1. Assembly exercise using plastic building blocks.

Jan has completed the Lean training overview with the team and it is now time to begin the work of building the model line. Let's listen in as Jan begins.

"The first thing we must determine is the rate of production. Do you remember the term we used to set the rate of production as we built the models?" Jan asked the team.

"Takt time," someone answers.

"Good, and how can we determine the Takt time for the value stream?"

"First, we have to know the demand, and then we have to know how much time we have available," Stan volunteers.

"Okay, where can we find this information?" Jan queries. Not getting an answer, Jan suggests, "It should be on the value stream map, shouldn't it? Our map shows that we ship an average of 5,000 units per week or 1,000 units per day. And in our future state map, we said that for now we would work only one shift. An eight-hour day has 480 minutes, but we have to take out the two 10-minute breaks and then a 15-minute clean-up period at the end of the day. So, that leaves 445 minutes. If you turn minutes into seconds, it means we have 26,700 seconds to produce the 1,000 units. Does anyone remember the calculation for Takt Time?"

Leanne, one member of the team, pours over her notes and offers, "We have to divide the available time by the demand."

"Great!" Jan encourages. "Calculating 26,000 seconds divided by 1,000 units is 26.7 seconds per unit. Just to make this easy for everyone to remember, let's round this up to 30 seconds. So the rate of production will need to be 30 seconds. The machinery used and the work content of everyone in the manufacturing process should match that Takt time or a multiple of it."

Stan interrupts. "But Jan, you and I talked about the fact that not every product runs at the same speed. After all, we are a job shop. We are not setting up an assembly line. We are talking in averages here. Does this mean that for a product that is normally run at 20 seconds per unit, we should all just work slower?"

"That's a great question, Stan, and there is no pat answer." Jan ponders a moment. "There are many possible solutions and we will explore some of these 'real time' as we move into the process. For now, I suggest that we use a modified hour-by-hour chart and let it help us pace the manufacturing processes."

First: rate of production
↳ takt time
↓
how determinate it?
for value stream?
. We have to know the demand
. available time

[...]harts, a new use for

e[...] ustomer, and single-

m[...]

H[...]

[...] Ann, another team

m[...]

[...] training. "Remem-

be[...] places it on the over-

head projector (see Figure 6-2). "The product we were making was very uniform in the speed at which we could build it. So, it was easy to plot on a straight-line linearity chart. In your case, The Jobbe Shoppe has products that run at different rates. We do not want the team to wait until the end of the day to find out if they are on track or not. I think that a modified linearity chart might work for this manufacturing cell. Here's an example," Jan continues. "Notice how the line is not straight, but varies depending on the product being produced. At different times of the day, the line is steeper and at other times the line is gradual. Notice also that there are times when the line is flat. What do you think this means?"

The team members look at each other, and finally Stan ventures a guess. "It looks like that flat line happens between parts. Could that be when the setup is happening?"

"Exactly," Jan says. "So planned setups and different run rates can be plotted on a modified hour-by-hour chart to guide the team's decision making" (see Figure 6-3.) "Again, the goal is to match the average Takt time for the hour and for the day. For example, if the team begins to overproduce and the plotted results for planned production are above the linearity chart by five percent, this might be the time to stop production. They could do something else such as preventive maintenance or some cross-training. When the production goal and time of day are realigned, then the team would begin to produce again.

"On the other hand, if the team finds itself producing below the line by more than five percent, they get the team together. They

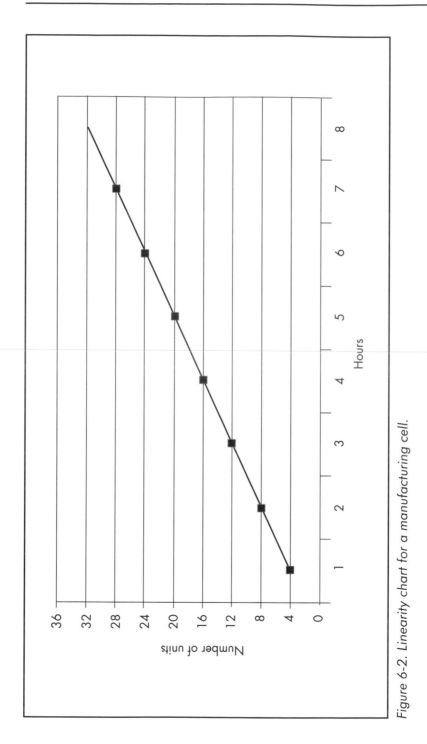

Figure 6-2. Linearity chart for a manufacturing cell.

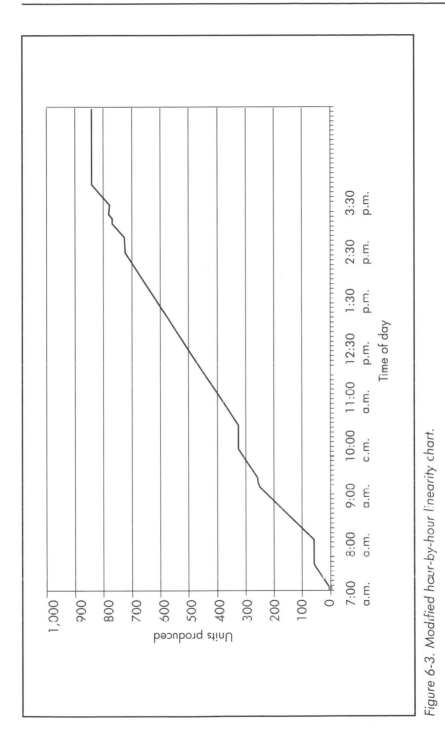

Figure 6-3. Modified hour-by-hour linearity chart.

can identify the problem, call in resources, or do whatever it takes to get things turned around before the end of the day. Once they begin making improvements to setup times and run rates, they can make changes to the spreadsheet that develops this hour-by-hour chart. That way the team can capitalize on its improvements."

A New Use for Economic Order Quantity

During Jan's team training, the team determined that setup time must be accounted for. The recommendation to follow may be viewed on the surface as heresy by any experienced advocates of the Lean approach. Please reserve judgement until the reasoning is explained. Every business school, Masters of Business Administration (MBA) program, and APICS: The Education Society for Resource Management course teaches the *economic order quantity* (EOQ) formula. This mathematical technique is used to determine the most financially rewarding lot size to build, given a couple of key criteria. The input criteria include interest rate (what it will cost to carry inventory) and setup cost (what it will cost to prepare to run the product).

Although Figure 6-4 greatly simplifies the concept of the EOQ, it graphically demonstrates how the intersecting lines and total cost of setup and carrying cost can help determine the optimum lot size. The EOQ would recommend the ideal lot size approximately where the lines cross and the total cost is lowest. As shown in Figure 6-4, the ideal number to build appears to be around 21 or 22 units. If we make many more than this, and hold the inventory, we will pay unnecessary storage costs. If we make less that this, we will pay too much for the setup.

On the surface it seems like a logical approach, but the problem with the EOQ is that it assumes setup costs are fixed, like carrying costs. In approximately 50 setup-reduction projects, it was found that setup times can nearly always be cut at least in half. Does this make the EOQ methodology null and void?

At some point, if you reduce setup times to the point of being insignificant, then the EOQ formula can be a waste of time. Depending on the unit cost, in a job shop anything less than 10 minutes approaches the realm of insignificance.   •

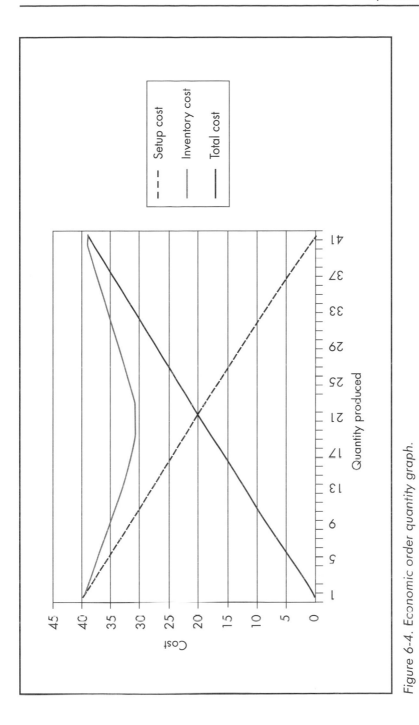

Figure 6-4. Economic order quantity graph.

What if you are just starting down the Lean path? Is there an interim use for the EOQ?

History has verified the folly of ignoring the opportunity hiding within the high cost of setup, but many managers neglect this gold mine. Therefore, a hybrid approach to the EOQ is required to make the cost of setups more visual. The next paragraphs describe the data required in spreadsheet form and the reason for each entry:

1. First, the EOQ formula requires an annual consumption or demand from the customer. This can be historical data if there is a lack of an accurate forecast.
2. Next, the sales price, or unit cost, is needed to calculate the EOQ accurately.
3. Third, the amount you pay for monies borrowed to store inventory is required. This should be expressed as a percentage.
4. Then, the total cost of setup (for all steps in the manufacturing process) should be entered. In this example, the labor cost of $10.00 is based on 40 minutes of setup time at $15.00 per hour (two-thirds of an hour being 40 minutes, two-thirds of $15.00 being $10.00).
5. Very important and often overlooked is the next data point, setup waste. If I throw away one piece at each step, and there are five steps, this needs to be evaluated as a part of my setup costs.
6. The cost to plan and release a job to the manufacturing floor is the next data point entered. In this case, let's assume that we have three planners and together their accumulated wage is $100,000 per year. If they each release an average of 277 work orders per month, or 3,333 per year, then each work order released is costing $10.00.
7. Next is the number of times the customer orders the part each year. In this case they would like to order it weekly (52 times annually).
8. Finally, estimate the percentage of confidence that the part will not change during the next year. If there is a good chance that revisions will occur, then enter a lower number. This is not a scientific number, but a number based on intuition and what is known about the customer, the market, and product life cycles.

Based on this discussion, the first eight fields of the EOQ spreadsheet are as follows:

Annual usage	10,000
Unit cost	$10.00
Carrying cost	10%
Setup cost	$10.00
Setup waste (in pieces)	5
Planning cost per order	$10.00
Order frequency per year	52
Probability of no revisions	100%

After they are filled in, the EOQ spreadsheet will provide you with key information you can use to make business decisions.

The EOQ formula based on the previous information recommends that due to the cost of planning, setup, and waste, it is better financially to produce the material only eight times per year. The line below shows the number to make each time the job is run. This will obviously result in inventory since the customer orders only 192 per week on average.

Recommended setups per year	8
Economic order quantity	1,183

Second, the financial benefit of utilizing the EOQ is shown. In this case, even though higher inventory carrying costs are accounted for, there is a $2,456 benefit to using the EOQ. There is also an additional benefit of a 1.9 percent capacity improvement.

You can begin to see why people trained in the use of EOQ are motivated to produce large batch sizes. On the surface, it makes perfect economic sense. But wait. What happens if we don't assume that setup costs are fixed? What if we could reduce the cost of setups, waste, and planning? Would there then be the same economic motivation to build large batches and hold inventory if these inputs were changed? Let's see.

Notice that the annual usage is the same, as is the unit cost, and carrying cost. However, let's say we are able to reduce setup time from 40 minutes to six minutes. Now it costs us $1.50 instead of $10.00. And let's also base this data on the assumption that we are able to reduce setup waste from five pieces to one. Additionally, if by using visual techniques (such as an empty shelf, box, tote bin, or cart) we can reduce the cost of planning an order by half, we can input $5.00 instead of $10.00 for planning costs.

The final two data points are the same as in the prior example: the customer still prefers to order weekly and there is 100 percent probability of no revisions. The revised EOQ spreadsheet:

Annual usage	10,000
Unit cost	$10.00
Carrying cost	10%
Setup cost	$1.50
Setup waste (in pieces)	1
Planning cost per order	$5.00
Order frequency per year	52
Probability of no revisions	100%

The EOQ spreadsheet now recommends that you build the product 17 times a year instead of only eight times. This is an improvement, but it does not meet the customer's need of 52 shipments. If we were able to continue to reduce the costs until the setup expenses were zero, we would see the EOQ formula result in a EOQ of 52 (once per month), just what the customer wants. But there will always be some setup costs. It is unrealistic to expect that we will eliminate all costs related to changeover. The important message here is that in the first example, the financial benefit of using the EOQ was nearly $2,500 per year per part number.

Recommended setups per year	17
Economic order quantity	574

In the second example, the financial benefits of building parts in 574-piece lot sizes are so small ($283.54) that it probably makes sense to manufacture them order-for-order, just as the customer wants.

Annual financial benefit of using EOQ	$283.54
Annual capacity improvement	1.5%

I hope the EOQ spreadsheet will make the cost of setups visible to everyone in your shop. Remember that the examples shown reflect the cost and benefits of only one part number. If your company was able to capitalize on a similar improvement for 100 part numbers over a year, the financial impact could be staggering.

Here is one more example of the EOQ concept. Look at Tables 6-1, 6-2, and 6-3. The tables compare the three primary ways of spending money on setups, which are:

1. Use the EOQ, hide setup costs, carry inventory,
2. Build lot-for-lot and absorb the cost of setups, or
3. Fix the setup.

Table 6-1 illustrates the cost of the first option, based on producing 100 similar part numbers. It will cost $115,161 every year to run the recommended EOQ and store an average of half the lot size (625 average units in inventory).

Table 6-2 shows the second option, the cost of running lot-for-lot on the same 100 part numbers. Although the inventory carrying costs are reduced, the overall effect is that it will cost nearly $250,000 more per year to run these 100 part numbers every week in lot sizes of 192 rather than 1,250.

The third option shown in Table 6-3 would spend $30,000 on improving or fixing the setup. Eliminating the setup time will certainly cost something. A team of five or six people working for a

Table 6-1. Setup costs worksheet, option 1

Cost Itemization	Use of EOQ Option 1
Unit cost	10.00
Annual order quantity	10,000
Average order size	1,250
Order frequency	8
Carrying cost (10%)	$591.61
Setup cost (per setup)	$10.00
Setup waste cost	$50.00
Planning cost per order	$10.00
Total annual setup costs	$560.00
Cost of improvements	$0.00
Total part numbers affected	100
1st year setup costs	$115,161.00
2nd year average cost	$115,161.00

Table 6-2. Setup cost worksheet, option 2

Cost Itemization	Use of EOQ Option 1	No Setup Reduction Option 2
Unit cost	10.00	10.00
Annual order quantity	10,000	10,000
Average order size	1,250	192
Order frequency	8	52
Carrying cost (10%)	$591.61	$9.60
Setup cost (per setup)	$10.00	$10.00
Setup waste cost	$50.00	$50.00
Planning cost per order	$10.00	$10.00
Total annual setup costs	$560.00	$3,640.00
Cost of improvements	$0.00	$0.00
Total part numbers affected	100	100
1st year setup costs	$115,161.00	$364,960.00
2nd year average cost	$115,161.00	$364,960.00

week, changing setup processes and behaviors (rather than buying new equipment), can reduce most setups by 50 percent in the first go-around. That will cost about $3,500 in labor. If another $1,500 is spent on parts (speed wrenches, quick release handles, tool carts, etc.), then you will have $5,000 invested. Table 6-3 uses a $30,000 "fix-the-setup" figure, which assumes that you might run six such projects.

Notice that the first year costs are not much different than the first option's EOQ costs. But in the second year, the financial benefit gets better. If every year you assign the same $30,000 budget and the same team approach to fixing the setups, it will just get better and better.

Re-educating the Customer

So, why focus on setup times? Because setup is the primary tool to becoming Lean. If you cannot do quick setups, it will be very expensive to try to implement the rest of the Lean manufacturing principles.

Table 6-3. Setup cost worksheet, option 3

Cost Itemization	Use of EOQ Option 1	No Setup Reduction Option 2	Fix the Setup Option 3
Unit cost	10.00	10.00	10.00
Annual order quantity	10,000	10,000	10,000
Average order size	1,250	192	192
Order frequency	8	52	52
Carrying cost (10%)	$591.61	$9.60	$9.60
Setup cost (per setup)	$10.00	$10.00	$1.50
Setup waste cost	$50.00	$50.00	$10.00
Planning cost per order	$10.00	$10.00	$5.00
Total annual setup costs	$560.00	$3,640.00	$858.00
Cost of improvements	$0.00	$0.00	$30,000.00
Total part numbers affected	100	100	100
1st year setup costs	$115,161.00	$364,960.00	$116,760.00
2nd year average cost	$115,161.00	$364,960.00	$86,760.00

Not all customers drive us to produce smaller batch sizes. Some still think they can save themselves money by ordering large batch lot sizes. This is our fault. For years, the idea of buying in bulk at a discount has appealed to the frugal homemaker and purchasing agent alike. Bulk warehouse stores are a testimony to our "bigger-is-cheaper" mentality. We need to re-educate customers to realize that we can make their product as economically in the lot sizes they really need, rather than some super-sized truckload they have to find a place to store, inventory, count, protect, and so on.

Imagine shopping for your family the way some purchasing agents look at shopping for the business. On the average, we all probably make 52 trips to the store every year to purchase the major items for our nutritional needs. Let's say that we spend an average of $100 per week on groceries. Using the old EOQ formula, we decide that we should only buy groceries twice a year. With the warehouse membership, we can buy big cans of creamed corn and lima beans and large bags of rolled oats at two-thirds the cost of supermarket prices! We enlist the help of our entire family to push the 15 shopping carts needed for all this food. Then, after running up the credit card to pay for the groceries, we rent a truck to transport the food home. We move little sister out of her room because we need a place to store it.

About three weeks into the program, the entire family is so tired of creamed corn, lima beans, and oatmeal that they start eating at fast food restaurants on the way home. After two months, the humidity has ruined 80 percent of the dry goods, and the cat has torn the labels off every third can, so we have no idea what we are opening.

You get the picture. You know that this is no way to run a family. But too often, this is how companies are run. Customers have been taught by vendors that buying large will save them money. Exorbitant setup times are the root cause of this long-held belief. We can change that idea.

If there were no setup time, we could make one of anything for no more than it would cost to make one thousand of the same part number. However, realistically, there will always be some setup time. Some OEMs have led the way in reducing setup time from hours to seconds. We can all learn from their example.

Single-minute Exchange of Die

Toyota has for years used the Single-minute Exchange of Die (SMED) approach, and thousands of others have successfully adopted that model. Job shops have unique differences that may make it financially difficult to reach this level of setup maturity. Techniques such as quick-release tooling, shot-pin alignment systems, and standard die height have proven to be beneficial for high-volume manufacturers and assembly line operations. But these can be quite expensive for a small mom-and-pop shop.

Most job shops could benefit by adopting a Single-digit Exchange of Die (SDED) methodology rather than the SMED approach. This means focusing setup reduction efforts until the average setup is less than 10 minutes, thus making virtually every setup insignificant. It would be very difficult (and expensive) to try to go from 40-minute setups to one minute. But nearly every 40-minute setup can be reduced to nine minutes or less.

There are certainly job shops where single-minute exchange of tooling is a common practice, and we can all learn to utilize such techniques when the financial benefit warrants the effort and expense. As with most things in life and in business, the key is balance and progress.

In summary, inventory management techniques such as manufacturing resource planning (MRP) have their place. APICS training is a macro-planning (big view) tool. They are powerful tools for calculating capacity requirements and for intelligently planning the acquisition of long lead-time buy-out items. We should never accept the current condition as an unchangeable fact of life. If at all possible, we should eliminate the need for long lead times.

Measured use of the EOQ is a better solution than going out of business because you have raced to apply small lot sizing before you have mastered the fundamentals.

7

Just-in-Time Techniques

This is the story of the ham bone.

A couple had been married only a week or two, just back from their honeymoon, and the new wife decided to make her new husband a special dinner. So, she went to the butcher shop and ordered a large "bone-in" ham. Hams like these can have quite big bones and this one had a large joint sticking out of one end. The young wife asked to borrow the husband's hacksaw to cut off the ball joint. Glad to oblige, the husband lent a hand, but questioned the reason for cutting off the end of the ham bone. The wife pondered for a moment, shrugged, and simply said that her mother had always cut it off and so she did too.

Time went by and the opportunity came for the husband to ask his new mother-in-law the question: "Why do you cut the end of the ham bone off before you cook it?" Again, he got a momentary blank stare and the same answer as before: "That's the way my mother always did it." Now the husband was on a mission to find the answer to this question. He visited Grandma on the pretense of cleaning her gutters, but in reality to seek the ultimate wisdom regarding ham bones. Finally, he was able to pose the nagging question: "Why do you cut the end of the ham bone off before you cook it?" Grandma shuffled into the kitchen and reached into the pantry to retrieve the explanation. She simultaneously satisfied the young husband's original question and unknowingly perplexed him with an even deeper mystery. "It doesn't fit in my pot," she explained as she hefted the 50-year-old cast-iron stewing pot.

The message in this story, of course, is that the young wife and her mother continued to carry out practices of the past, even though the conditions may have changed. People do this every day, in life and in business. The "ham bone mentality" of carrying on outdated practices as if they were law can hold us back.

This chapter will introduce you to a toolbox that you can use to change the way you do business. It will require you and your team to think "outside the box," to forget the old, and to dream about the new. Setting aside the honored traditions of the past can be hard for some people, even if they are not the originators. If we have worked within a set of procedures and guidelines for a long time, we have a certain amount of ownership in the process. Ham bone thinking becomes less of a barrier to change when we ask ourselves to surrender this ownership.

The place to start is with the fundamentals: simple, direct, logical, without need of definition, basic principles keep the message clear and concise.

Think back to the wagon in Chapter 2. Notice that in Figure 7-1, one of the wheels, or business principles, is titled Lean Manufacturing Techniques. The 18 spokes on that wheel were shown in Figure 2-8.

The spokes on each wheel, which symbolize the key indicators, are different in number and in meaning. Keep in mind that the wheels and spokes of your organization will look different than the wheels and spokes of any other.

Some of the spokes are fundamental. This chapter will address these fundamental indicators one by one. To get started, let's modify the Lean manufacturing wheel so that it reflects only the

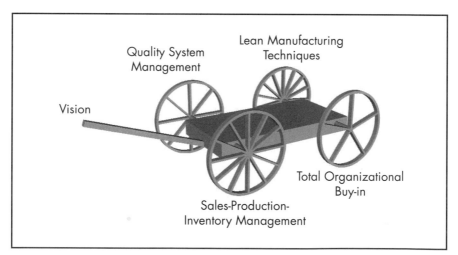

Figure 7-1. Lean enterprise vehicle.

ten primary tools to be discussed throughout this chapter. Figure 7-2 shows these ten primary techniques.

SMED—THE FAST SETUP TOOLBOX

Hopefully, Chapter 6 convinced you that ignoring the high cost of setups will lead to many forms of waste. A hybrid version of the Economic Order Quantity (EOQ) was introduced to determine lot sizes until the Single-Digit Exchange of Dies (SDED) approach was mastered. In the process, thousands of dollars may be saved.

This chapter will show you the tools for reducing setup times and describe a case study demonstrating the potential of such an approach. The process is simple:

1. Observe,
2. Brainstorm,
3. Improve, and
4. Test.

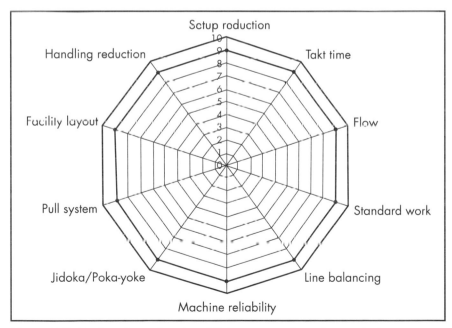

Figure 7-2. Radar chart showing 10 Lean manufacturing techniques.

The SMED methodology perfected in the automotive industry is used in job shops of all sizes and descriptions. Start by gathering all the forms referred to in this process, such as the setup observations sheet, the setup observation bar chart, and the spaghetti diagram.

Videotaping

Buy, borrow, or rent a video camera. Some consultants shy away from the videotape method, but there is strong evidence for its use. Operators often do not see some aspects of the setup during the observation. Plan to videotape a setup, but do not allow the operator(s) to stage tooling, material, paperwork, or anything else that would not ordinarily be staged ahead of time. Select a setup that is representative of the setups performed in the model line. It could be one that is particularly problematic or long, but try to avoid a setup that is still being perfected. The selection should also be one that has proven capability and will run regularly though the model line.

On the day of the setup, set the camera in a location that does not impede the operator, yet is close enough to capture all the movements within the machine area. If the operator needs to walk off camera to retrieve a tool, don't worry about following him/her. It is ideal to assign a camera operator and have him/her zoom in and out while capturing each setup activity in detail. Try to capture at least 10 minutes of the machine running prior to and after the setup. This will show what pre-setup and post-setup activities are happening ahead of or after the changeover. If possible, assign a two- or three-person team to observe the setup and document the steps taken. They should be close enough to the operator to ask clarifying questions, but not so close as to interfere with the operator. The observers should have a stopwatch and clipboards with setup observation sheets (see Tables 7-1 and 7-2). Things to note:

- If the setup requires more than one person, assign additional team(s) to observe the additional setup participants.

Table 7-1. One type of setup observation sheet

Step	Setup Reduction Project	Clock
1	Turn machine off	0.67
2	Count material	1.33
3	Ticket load	1.97
4	Find supervisor for next job	2.40
5	Complete paperwork from last job	6.95
6	Review blueprints for next job	8.53
7	Remove tooling	9.53
8	Store tooling	10.53
9	Clean machine	10.90
10	Push out material for forklift driver	11.90
11	Find forklift driver	12.25
12	Get setup sheet from notebook	12.55
13	Review setup sheet	12.82
14	Retrieve tooling	13.18
15	Install tooling	19.63
16	Program CNC	20.88
17	Help forklift driver	21.33
18	Fill out paperwork	21.83
19	Retrieve special backstop from toolbox	22.58
20	Test first part	24.83
21		
22		
23		
24		
25		
26		
27		
28		

- After the initial observation, the entire team, including the operator, should watch the videotape together.
- Develop a setup observation bar chart describing each setup component in graphical form (see Figure 7-3). This tool is used to make the time of each setup activity visible.

Table 7-2. Another type of setup observation sheet

Step	Setup Reduction Project	Element	Clock
1	Turn machine off	0.67	0.67
2	Count material	0.67	1.33
3	Ticket load	0.63	1.97
4	Find supervisor for next job	0.43	2.40
5	Complete paperwork from last job	4.55	6.95
6	Review blueprints for next job	1.58	8.53
7	Remove tooling	1.00	9.53
8	Store tooling	1.00	10.53
9	Clean machine	0.37	10.90
10	Push out material for forklift driver	1.00	11.90
11	Find forklift driver	0.35	12.25
12	Get setup sheet from notebook	0.30	12.55
13	Review setup sheet	0.27	12.82
14	Retrieve tooling	0.37	13.18
15	Install tooling	6.45	19.63
16	Program CNC	1.25	20.88
17	Help forklift driver	0.45	21.33
18	Fill out paperwork	0.50	21.83
19	Retrieve special backstop from toolbox	0.75	22.58
20	Test first part	2.25	24.83
21	Measure first part	0.32	25.15
22	Adjust controller	0.50	25.65
23	Test second part	0.37	26.02
24	Measure second part	0.50	26.52
25	Find cardboard to put on pallet	1.40	27.92
26	Count incoming material	1.10	29.02
27	Perform quality assurance (QA) on incoming material	0.35	29.37
28	Fill out QA paperwork	1.50	30.87

- If a third person is available, this person should come prepared with a sketch of the area, and during the setup, mark each movement of the operator with a line showing his/her travel. This will become the *spaghetti diagram* (see Figure 7-4). Alternatively, you can do the spaghetti diagram from the video.

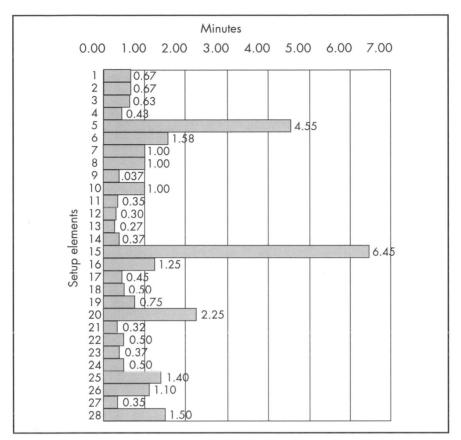

Figure 7-3. Setup observation bar chart.

Have the person with the stopwatch call out the clock time only at the beginning of each new activity or process step (see Table 7-1). This will save the team from having to perform time calculations for each step as they are trying to observe. Perform the time calculations for each setup element later, or enter the data into a spreadsheet and let it calculate for you.

Table 7-2 shows the calculation for each elemental time. The setup observation chart shown in Figure 7-3 graphically demonstrates that there are a few major setup activities consuming the majority of the setup time. These may hold the greatest opportunity, but don't be tempted to focus only on the two or three longest bars. Some teams go after the easy tasks and ignore the rest.

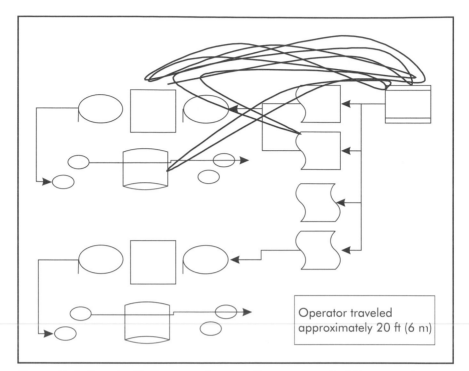

Figure 7-4. Spaghetti diagram showing the movement of the operator.

The way to cut overall setup time in half is to cut each setup component in half. If you do this for each individual setup activity, total setup will be reduced by 50 percent before you realize it. The only way to do this is to make each activity visible. This is the strength of the observation sheet. By using these graphs and tables as before and after comparisons, the team can be encouraged to focus on holding the gains.

Brainstorming

The next step is brainstorming, and for most people this is the fun part. The goal is to gather as many ideas as possible but to avoid qualifying or problem-solving as the ideas are gathered. There are no bad ideas; everyone has the same rank, and everyone is treated with dignity. Don't allow only the experts to offer ideas. Ask the non-experts for their opinions.

Setup Reduction

For each bar on the chart in Figure 7-3, try to think of at least three or four alternative ways the task might be done. The idea is to eliminate steps. If a step cannot be eliminated, then how could the task be made external to the setup? *External activities* are those actions that the operator or someone else can do before or after the machine is in setup mode.

Maybe you have heard of setups referred to as a *pit stop*. A race car can cost millions of dollars per year to buy and maintain. When a race team takes a car to the track, the goal is to keep it on the track as long as the race is underway. If the pit crew waits until the car is in the pit to begin putting air in the tires or fuel in the gas can, they are sure to lose the race.

Many companies have invested millions of dollars in their "race car," the equipment in the shop. It is common sense to ensure that when that kind of investment is made, time is of the essence when it comes to maximum efficiency.

Pit crews focus on every detail before, during, and after the pit stop. They are never satisfied with the status-quo. They videotape themselves and they brainstorm solutions to problems that might be keeping them from competing with other pit crews. The pit crew focuses on the quality of their work because lives are at stake. Seconds, rather than minutes, and a minimum of motion and effort are their common goals.

The activities performed by the pit crew are mostly external. Nothing is added or changed on the race car while it is still on the track. The internal activities begin only after the machine or race car stops rolling. If we look at the bar chart shown in Figure 7-3, we can begin the process of identifying which items might be considered the easiest tasks; those that might be done externally from the setup. Table 7-3 shows this work completed. According to the internal time left over, what was previously a 30-minute setup could theoretically be done in less than 14.44 minutes. This is if the operator was assisted by a pit crew performing all the external activities identified by the letter "E." The operator activities are shown with the letter "I."

The process should not stop here. Each activity can be streamlined to ensure that it is being done as smoothly and efficiently as

Table 7-3. Revised setup observation sheet with externalized activities identified

Step	Setup Reduction Project	Internal (I) /External (E)	Element	Clock
1	Turn machine off	I	0.67	0.67
2	Count material	E	0.67	
3	Ticket load	E	0.63	
4	Find supervisor for next job	E	0.43	
5	Complete paperwork from last job	E	4.55	
6	Review blueprints for next job	I	1.58	2.25
7	Remove tooling	I	1.00	3.25
8	Store tooling	E	1.00	
9	Clean machine	I	0.37	3.62
10	Push out material for forklift driver	E	1.00	
11	Find forklift driver	E	0.35	
12	Get setup sheet from notebook	E	0.30	
13	Review setup sheet	E	0.27	
14	Retrieve tooling	E	0.37	
15	Install tooling	I	6.45	10.07
16	Program CNC	I	1.25	11.32
17	Help forklift driver	E	0.45	
18	Fill out paperwork	E	0.50	
19	Retrieve backstop from toolbox	E	0.75	
20	Test first part	I	2.25	13.57
21	Measure first part	E	0.32	
22	Adjust controller	I	0.50	14.07
23	Test second part	I	0.37	14.44
24	Measure second part	E	0.50	
25	Find cardboard to put on pallet	E	1.40	
26	Count incoming material	E	1.10	
27	Perform QA on incoming material	E	0.35	
28	Fill out QA paperwork	E	1.50	

possible. Even though an activity is moved to external, it is still important to manage the labor applied to that activity. This describes the third step: improve.

Reducing Time

So far in our example, the potential for a 14.44-minute setup doesn't come from reducing the time it takes to complete any particular setup task. This is only the benefit of reassigning the work to someone who can do it away from the machine. While this does reduce downtime, the benefit of cutting each setup activity in half will reduce this 14.44-minute setup to less than eight minutes.

Testing the Solution

The fourth and final step is to test the solution. There is no better way to measure the value of an idea than to give it a try. If at all possible, try to use the same part number to perform the setup again. If this is not possible, try to select a part that is similar enough to measure the effect of all the improvement ideas (you may have to artificially duplicate the need for the setup by saving a couple of parts from the first test).

During the test, videotape the setup again and perform the same setup observation as in Table 7-1. This will provide the team with a clear comparison, a record of the improvement, and a training tool for future setup reduction teams.

If the tests prove effective and if the team adopts the new process, you can use the observation sheet as a beginning point for documenting and developing a *best practice* for all future setups. Try keeping a diary of all setup reduction projects, because sharing examples and case studies with new teammates, customers, and others is a powerful device for leading people toward the Lean approach.

Figures 7-5, 7-6, and 7-7 are examples from a case study. These are real results of a setup reduction project at a precision sheet metal company. The product was a very complicated and large panel component used in a blood analysis unit. The setup process being improved was related to a machine used to install or press in hardware (for example, nuts, screws, and standoffs). With more than six different kinds of hardware and over 20 individual pieces, the operation was prone to quality problems and long setup times. Studies showed that it took about three hours per order to perform all the setups for all the hardware on these parts. When the

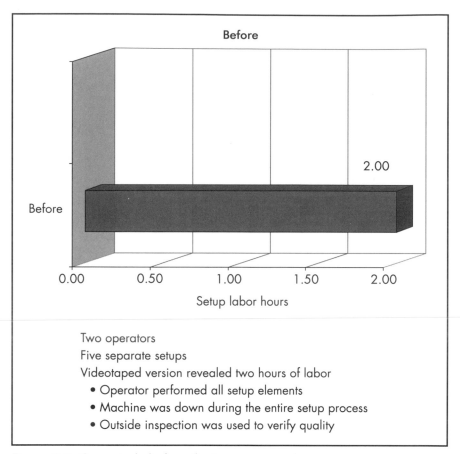

Figure 7-5. Case study before the Lean approach.

team was videotaped, the time was about two hours. So, there appeared to be an immediate improvement due to the "Hawthorne effect" (just because we were there).

There are many good books available on setup reduction. Another good resource for finding setup reduction techniques is trade association seminars and workshops.

CALCULATING TAKT TIMES

Not much space will be used to define *Takt time* in this book. A lot has been written on this subject and suffice it to say that Takt

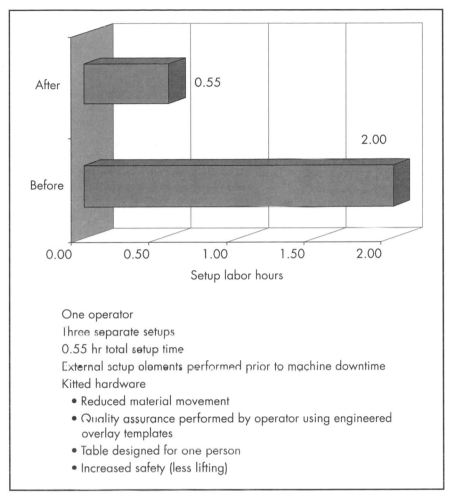

Figure 7-6. Case study after the Lean approach.

time is a tool. The word is of German origin and relates to rhythm. Like a music conductor's baton, Takt time is a tool by which you can set the pace or beat of a manufacturing process.

Think about Takt time as your heartbeat. Your heartbeat should be steady and consistent, regardless of the activity. When your activity increases, your heartbeat should increase, but it would not be good if it were erratic or unstable. People die of arrhythmia, an uncontrollable fluctuation in heart rate. In business, there

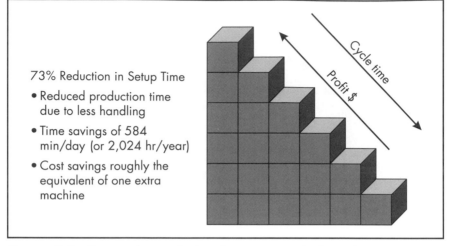

73% Reduction in Setup Time
- Reduced production time due to less handling
- Time savings of 584 min/day (or 2,024 hr/year)
- Cost savings roughly the equivalent of one extra machine

Figure 7-7. Economic analysis of a case study based on an entire department's improvement.

are often seasonal cycles in product sales. Shorter and shorter product life cycles mean capacity planning and material procurement skills are put to the test every day.

The heartbeat analogy fits well with the reality of business. You want to be able to ramp up the heartbeat of your business (production) in relationship to the demand. But if you do not have a target heartbeat (rate of production) that everyone in the body (value stream or model line) can feel and get in time with, then everyone is trying to produce to their own beat. Obviously, this is not a good situation.

Establishing two or three Takt times for the primary demand patterns is critical. One analogy describing the differing levels of Takt time is a three-speed transmission. The greater the demand for speed, the greater the demand for a higher gear. For simplicity in the rest of this discussion, the three demand patterns will be described as light, moderate, and heavy.

An assembly line that has two, three, four, or even a half dozen major part numbers, each with multiple variations, can make use of the TOP approach: Takt time, one-piece flow, and pull. TOP can be applied in a job shop where the manufacturing processes are well established and there are moderately sound forecasts and product repeatability. However, to dogmatically hold that TOP is the only approach to being Lean is not reasonable. There must be some room for flexibility in the typical job shop environment of miserable forecasts and thousands of unique part numbers.

The methodology of TOP and the Toyota production system is sound and the techniques are flawless when applying them to assembly processes or high-volume manufacturing. But, a job shop dealing with 3,500 active part numbers, none of which are adequately forecasted by the customer, will have a much harder time developing precise Takt times, flawless flow patterns, or perfect pull systems. The approach will only work if it is modified for the job shop environment. So, the task is to develop a hybrid system that allows smaller companies to retain the nimble nature that makes them so attractive to customers who need low volume, one-of-a-kind products, or proto-typing services, while at the same time meeting the needs of customers who order on a more routine basis.

Stan and Jan will need to calculate three levels of Takt time for their model line. But, it is hard to calculate Takt times for prototyping services. There are too many variables and life isn't long enough. Instead of trying to apply Takt time to 100 percent of the product in the job shop, they resolved to focus on the 80–20 rule and be good at pacing the shop for the 80 percent bread-and-butter product lines.

Takt times are used for those processes that fit the mold of being moderately repetitive, proven, capable, and stable. Who said that Takt time had to be used for every product, every day, every month, every year? Isn't continuous improvement about breaking the mold, losing the ham bone mentality, and thinking outside the box? What's wrong with running to a defined Takt time four days out of five (or six hours out of eight), and then using the last part of the day or week for prototyping, or for those one-of-a-kind items (what we call "dogs and cats")? Or how about a weekend shift running to Takt time and dealing with all the proven high-volume product? This would allow the miscellaneous material to flow during the week when experienced personnel are available to answer questions.

Think outside the box. There has to be an answer other than the hard and fast rule that says; "It's Takt time, one-piece flow, and pull, or it's nothing." Takt time is a tool, one tool of many, and it has its place. Our model line will definitely use it, but don't let dogmatic consultants force TOP where it doesn't fit or before you are ready for it.

If the average monthly order quantity during a moderate sales period is 20,000 units and you plan to run the manufacturing cell eight hours per day, five days per week, you can adjust for any slight variation in demand by working fewer or more hours per day, or by working fewer or more days per week. DO NOT change the Takt time unless there are significant and sustained changes to the demand pattern. And then do not change it arbitrarily. Have a predetermined Takt time calculated so that everyone can get in rhythm with the new heartbeat. This will be discussed in greater detail when we talk about standard work.

Notice that in Table 7-4, the average monthly demand is 20,000 units for four different product types. The result is an average Takt time of one unit every 1.8 minutes (or 108 seconds). This is not simply the average Takt time of each product's Takt time added together and divided by four. To ensure accuracy, the sales percentage (54 percent) or the percentage of time the product needs to run at 0.8 minutes per unit (on Product ABC) need to be part of the computation. Therefore, performing this calculation produces the number 1.8. The following was obtained by multiplying the percent of total sales times the Takt time for each product (see Table 7-4). Takt time for the average monthly demand can also be expressed as:

$$T_t = \text{the product of } (T_m S_p) \hspace{2cm} (7\text{-}1)$$

where:

T_t = Takt time
T_m = time in minutes it takes to make the product
S_p = percent of total sales per month

Therefore:

$(0.8 \times 54\%)$ ABC product $= 0.432$
$(1.8 \times 25\%)$ XYZ product $= 0.450$
$(3.3 \times 13\%)$ LMN product $= 0.429$
$(5.9 \times 8\%)$ FGH product $= \underline{0.472}$
$$T_t = 1.8$$

Table 7-4. Takt time for average monthly demand

Moderate Demand Takt Time	Product ABC	Product XYZ	Product LMN	Product FGH	Total
Annual demand	130,000	60,000	32,000	18,000	240,000
Monthly demand	10,833	5,000	2,667	1,500	20,000
Daily demand	542	250	133	75	1,000
Percent of total sales	54%	25%	13%	8%	
Takt time (min/unit)	0.8	1.8	3.3	5.9	1.8*
Operator cycle time					
Ideal number of operator					

*See Equation 7-1

We will come back to the two rows not completed in Table 7-4 later, operator cycle time and ideal number of operators.

What does a 1.8-minute Takt time mean to Stan and Jan as they set up their model line back at The Jobbe Shoppe? It means they will need to ensure that all the equipment is capable of producing not only to 1.8 minute cycle times, but to the lowest listed Takt time (0.8). Otherwise, there could be a bottleneck in the process.

Table 7-4 showed the Takt time for a moderate demand pattern. Table 7-5 shows the same spreadsheet for the same product, but includes additional information related to crewing. Table 7-6 shows the result of a light demand pattern.

The heavy demand pattern shown in Table 7-7 reveals that instead of one unit every 1.8 minutes, the pace is one unit every 1.5 minutes. The light demand pattern shown in Table 7-6 results in a Takt time of 2.3 minutes per unit. These changes may seem minor, but everything about the manufacturing environment must be designed to allow this to happen, and the team must be able to staff itself (apply an effective number of people) for all three potential paces. If the team cannot adjust the size of the crew and has to run at a slower Takt time with the same number of people, it doesn't take a financial expert to see that money would be lost.

GETTING THE PROCESS TO FLOW

If you intend to produce to Takt time, then the flow of the product must be smooth and uninterrupted by transportation issues, staging areas, or work-in-process (WIP) inventory. Therefore, the next technique we need to apply is flow. This is as easy as asking yourself one question: "What causes the material to stop moving?" It is generally one of the following: distance, handling method, setup time of one or more machines in the value stream, or machines not meeting the required rate of production due to unplanned downtime, breakdown, or lack of capability.

Just as there might be many possible reasons for nonflow or back flow, there are many steps you can take to avoid doing nothing. Perfect examples of one-piece flow exist in automotive assembly plants, but job shops must remain flexible. You may need interim solutions until the right size equipment is available, or the schedule can be smoothed, or machines are capable, or people

Table 7-5. Takt time for a higher demand pattern

Moderate Demand Takt Time	Product ABC	Product XYZ	Product LMN	Product FGH	Total
Annual demand	130,000	60,000	32,000	18,000	240,000
Monthly demand	10,833	5,000	2,567	1,500	20,000
Daily demand	542	250	133	75	1,000
Percent of total sales	54%	25%	13%	8%	
Takt time (min/unit)	0.8	1.8	3.3	5.9	1.8*
Operator cycle time	4.5	3.0	2.5	6.0	4.0
Ideal number of operators	5.5	1.7	0.7	1.0	3.6

*See Equation 7-1

Table 7-6. Takt time for light demand pattern

Light Demand Takt Time	Product ABC	Product XYZ	Product LMN	Product FGH	Total
Percent sales fluctuate	-25%	-20%	-10%	-30%	
Annual demand	97,500	43,000	28,800	12,600	18,690
Monthly demand	8,125	4,000	2,400	1,050	15,575
Daily demand	406	200	120	53	778
Percent of total sales	52%	26%	15%	7%	
Takt time (min/unit)	1.1	2.2	3.7	8.5	2.3*
Operator cycle time					
Ideal number of operators					

*See Equation 7-1

Table 7-7. Takt time for heavy demand pattern

Heavy Demand Takt Time	Product ABC	Product XYZ	Product LMN	Product FGH	Total
Percent sales fluctuate	25%	15%	30%	10%	
Annual demand	162,500	69,000	41,600	19,800	292,900
Monthly demand	13,542	5,750	3,467	1,650	24,408
Daily demand	677	288	173	83	1,220
Percent of total sales	55%	24%	14%	7%	
Takt time (min/unit)	0.7	1.5	2.6	5.4	1.5*
Operator cycle time					
Ideal number of operators					

*See Equation 7-1

are trained, or bottlenecks are eliminated. Do not allow problems or challenges to delay getting started. Doing nothing until perfection is within grasp is a sure way of seeing more aggressive companies pass you by.

One-unit flow, one-pallet flow, or one-container flow is better than no flow at all. The secret is to never be satisfied with the current condition. Keep seeking to match the Takt time, improve the process, reduce the move quantity, shorten the distance, and perfect the delivery system until an ideal flow pattern is attained. Don't pass up the gains by waiting for one-piece flow.

In preparation for developing standard work, you will need to calculate how many operators are needed at each of the three different Takt times. This can be a "chicken-or-the-egg situation." You need the operator cycle time, but how can you make job assignments if you don't know how many people are required, and you can't know how many people you need if you don't know the operator cycle time, etc. To make this simple, here is a formula to determine the number of operators needed:

$$O = C_t \div T'_t \qquad\qquad (7\text{-}2)$$

where:

O = the total number of operators needed
C_t = operator cycle time
T_t = Takt time

This formula was used to calculate the number of operators needed in Table 7-5. The result indicates 3.6 people are required for this product mix, at these sales volumes, and using the operator cycle times provided. Of course, there is no such thing as six-tenths of a person, so always round up until you can make improvements to reduce operator cycle times. You can then reassign one person to another value stream.

So, where did we get the data for entering the operator cycle times in Table 7-5? That will be discussed in the next section.

One more point before we leave the issue of calculating the ideal number of operators in a process: when the Takt time changes, expect to add or delete team personnel. For example, an increase in sales volume will change the Takt time from 1.8 minutes per unit to 1.5 minutes; this will require 4.5 people (round up to 5). Conversely, a decrease in sales volume will change the Takt time to 2.3 minutes per unit and require 2.9 people (round up to three). You can now begin to see why the flexibility of our model line layout is so important.

STANDARD WORK

Think back to the analogy of the race car in the setup reduction discussion. The racing team performing all the activities in the pit stop must have an action plan to accomplish their tasks as efficiently as possible. If one of the team members fails to complete a task it could not only cost them the race, but it could be potentially life threatening. Every step must be planned and organized in the sequence needed. You can also be sure that the pit crew does not wait until the day of the race to discuss their action plan or to practice. In a work cell, the action plan is no less important. We call this assignment of tasks *standard work*. Practice makes perfect, so a work team should feel obligated to document and perfect the standard work until it becomes routine.

There are countless ways to gather the information necessary for developing standard work. To keep this simple, I will describe only one method, a process that has proved to be very effective. The process can be modified to fit your needs.

Line balancing and standard work are very closely related and we will discuss both in this section. We will develop what I call "dance cards" (standard work) for the moderate Takt time shown in Tables 7-4 and 7-5. The process is repeated for both higher demand and lower demand Takt times, although Step 1 will already be done. The process is simple:

1. Observe and document each activity.
2. Match each activity to an operator.
3. Distribute the work so that every operator has approximately the same amount.
4. Make sure each operator cycle time matches the Takt time.
5. Document each operator's tasks and develop dance cards.
6. Repeat the process for each Takt time.

Here are the tools you will need:

- Assorted colored felt pens,
- Notepads (recipe cards work well),

- Stopwatch,
- Clipboard,
- Cycle-time observation sheet,
- A blank wall, 10 to 20 ft (3 to 6 m) long, and
- Teams of two people to observe each operator.

In the following example, we are observing the process of manufacturing the product, not the setup. Having dance cards developed for the setup is also a good idea, but for now, let's not confuse the two. The objective is to observe and record the time it takes to complete one entire cycle at each process step. Since we are looking for an average, we will time each cycle at least 10 times. Some operators are faster than others and some products run faster than others. We are looking for the average, not perfection, at this point. Do not fret over the fact that there is opportunity for variation. We are just seeking a beginning point.

Table 7-8 shows the observation form. Notice that the lower right corner is where the "lowest repeatable cycle time" is entered. This is the number assigned to each operation element. Table 7-9 shows the form partially filled in.

As with the setup reduction observations, do not try to calculate the individual elements while performing the observations. Notice that the bold numbers are the stopwatch running times. The numbers directly beneath the bold numbers are the elapsed time for each step. The elapsed times can be calculated after the observation is complete. The total time for each cycle is listed at the bottom of each column. If something out of the ordinary happens, such as a machine breakdown, do not use this as a data point.

There are only ten rows provided in Table 7-9. This is by design. Ten steps are usually enough if you break down each distinct activity (load punch, deburr edges, etc.) on a separate sheet. The reason to separate each activity onto a separate sheet is to make it easier to distribute individual tasks as a part of line balancing. If you need more than ten line items, you can modify this form to suit your needs.

A second reason to observe the process is to identify any operation that could prove to be a potential bottleneck. Table 7-9 shows the lowest repeatable cycle time thus far to be 46 seconds. This is well below the shortest Takt time of 1.5 minutes as calculated for the heavy demand pattern shown in Table 7-7.

Table 7-8. Example of observation form

Process Step	Operation Element	Observer									Date	Task Time	Comments
		1	2	3	4	5	6	7	8	9	10		
1													
2													
3													
4													
5													
6													
7													
8													
9													
10													
	Cycle time>>												<<Lowest repeatable cycle time

Table 7-9. Observation form, partially filled in

Observer: Gus   Date: 10-Feb-00

Process Step	Operation Element	Turret Punching 1	2	3	4	5	6	7	8	9	10	Task Time	Comments
1	Unload machine	:08 / 8	:53 / 7	— / 8	—							8	
2	Load machine	:18 / 10	— / 11	— / 10	—							10	
3	File edges	:20 / 2	— / 2	— / 3	—							2	
4	Measure part	:30 / 10	— / 9	— / 10	—							10	
5	Wipe down part	:33 / 3	— / 3	— / 4	—							3	
6	Stack part	:43 / 9	— / 9	— / 9	—							9	
7	Prepare next part	:46 / 3	— / 3	— / 2	—							3	
8													
9													
10													
	Cycle time>>	46	44	46								46	<<Lowest repeatable cycle time

If any operation proves incapable of meeting the Takt time, then before they go any further, the team should problem solve a way to relieve the bottleneck. If the team cannot find a way to speed up the process to match the Takt time, then they need to explore options such as temporarily adding a second machine or operation of the same type. They may choose to run the process through lunch or breaks, or, as a last resort, add a second shift to build a daily stock of standard WIP until improvements can be found.

Once each step has been recorded and collected, define each separate activity by a simple title. Record each one onto sticky notes along with the lowest repeatable cycle time.

LINE BALANCING

The goal of *line balancing* is to make sure that every person in the manufacturing team has approximately the same amount of work during each manufacturing cycle. Figure 7-8 shows an example of a process that is out of balance. Operator four would have too much work to do while operators five and six would always be waiting for something to do. Like a relay race, each person must have an equal and balanced share of work.

Find a blank wall. Gather together all the cards for the process steps and divide the wall into the same number of operators staffing the model line. The objective is to distribute the notes below each operator's name, ensuring that each person has approximately the same amount of work. The amount of work for each person should match the Takt time as closely as possible. Figure 7-8 demonstrates the need to balance the workload. If any one operator has more work than the Takt time allows, the team will always be late. If there is too little to do, he/she will always be waiting for parts, and in the process, losing efficiency and getting frustrated.

Just like the pit crew discussed earlier, the way to avoid confusion and workload imbalances is not to wait until the day of the race to make the teams' work assignments. The work assignment wall should begin to look like Figure 7-9.

Once all the work assignments are made and you have made sure that each operator cycle time closely matches the Takt time, record each operator's work steps on a standard work combina-

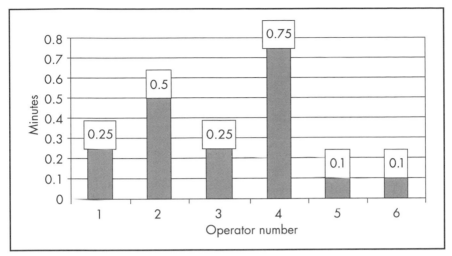

Figure 7-8. Graph showing the need for balanced operator cycle times.

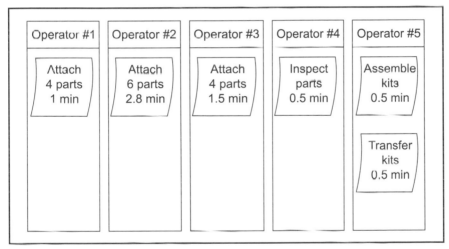

Figure 7-9. Work assignment exercise.

tion sheet (shown in the next section). However, before the team is done, they need to develop standard work for the other two Takt times. There is a tendency to skip this step or wait, but think about what will happen if the order file (sales) falls off or picks up. Don't put off until tomorrow what you won't have time for tomorrow either. If you wait until the last minute, there will be no time to test the process and make adjustments. Ignoring the need to change Takt times could also result in higher than required levels of finished goods.

Figure 7-10 shows an example of how work assignments might be rearranged for a light load, where the Takt time might be three minutes per unit instead of 1.5 minutes as shown in Figure 7-9.

Although facilities layout will be discussed at the end of this chapter, some thought must be given at this point to the physical arrangement of the cell. If the team is going to be able to distribute a larger or smaller number of people among the operations according to the three demand patterns, the distance traveled between these operations must allow a person to perform redefined duties without having to run from place to place.

Fluctuation in sales orders is a fact of life in the job shop. This may require temporarily moving part of the team to another value stream until orders pick up. Yet, it is not healthy for a team to have its members tossed to and fro at every whim of the customer. What is the solution? Even though you will have a Takt time and standard work for different sales levels, try to control the minor

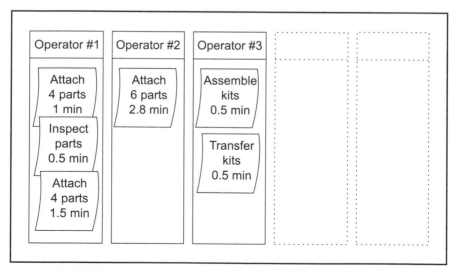

Figure 7-10. Work assignment rearranged for light load.

variations by adjusting hours worked rather than running people in and out of the model line.

It takes time to develop a rhythm or Takt time. If the Takt time changes every day or week, it would be like members of a band all playing songs at a different rhythms. No one would be able to keep track of the correct pace, and the music would sound terrible.

The solution is to plan for the need to adjust Takt time. When the adjustment happens, the transition will be easier and more efficient if the team has modified *standard work combination sheets* they can use to direct themselves. This is also a great training tool when new people join the team. A third purpose for the exercise is to provide clear cross-training outlines. Having team members out on vacation or out sick can be devastating if other team members cannot pick up a standard work combination sheet and fill in for the absence.

Figure 7-11 shows a blank standard work combination sheet. Figure 7-12 shows how it looks after work content is filled in. You can be as detailed or as simple as you wish with these forms. The key is to be clear about the expectations. In addition to standard work combinations, you might include a list of duties that can be done in cases of breakdown, material shortages, etc.

MACHINE RELIABILITY

One of the most powerful and memorable visual images relating to the Lean implementation or world-class approach is of a boat floating over a body of water. Look at Figure 7-13. The boat symbolizes the business. The water symbolizes all forms of inventory: raw material, work-in-process, and finished goods. The rocks symbolize problems or barriers. The objective is, of course, to have smooth sailing, free-flowing water, and no obstructions. The inventory protects the boat from hidden rocks. Lowering the water level (the inventory) exposes previously unseen rocks (problems) and the boat (the business) is sure to crash into them.

The choice is a simple: either ignore the Lean approach and raise the water level to hide the rocks again, or use the techniques described here to remove the rocks. An easy choice to talk about, but harder to implement. This is where the commitment to the Lean approach is tested at the highest level of the organization.

Date		Work sequence				Quota	
Part name						Takt time	
Step #	Work content	Manual time	Automatic time	Walk time			

Figure 7-11. Standard work combination sheet.

Date		Work sequence			Quota = 600/shift
Part name					Takt time = 0.76 min or 46 sec

Legend:
- ■ = manual
- ▨ = automatic
- ■ = walking
- ▨ = waiting

Step	Work content	Manual time	Automatic time	Walk time
1	Unload drill	5	—	—
2	Load/start drill	3	15	2
3	Degrease part	7		
4	Unload/load weld	7	14	2
5	Unload lathe	7	—	—
6	Load and start lathe	5	16	2
7	Return to drill	—	—	3
8				
9				
Total		34		9

= 43 sec OCT

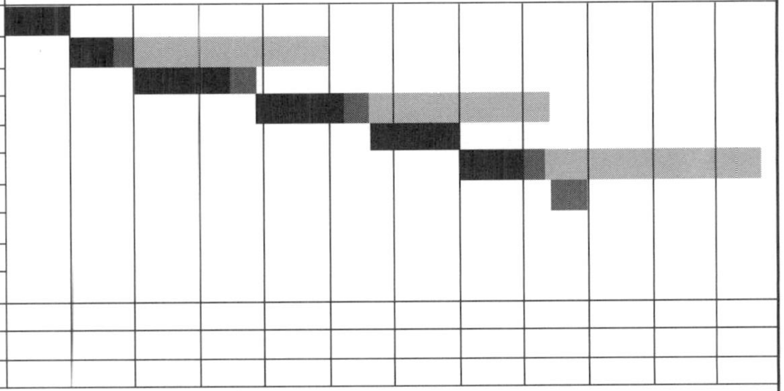

Figure 7-12. Partially filled in standard work combination sheet.

107

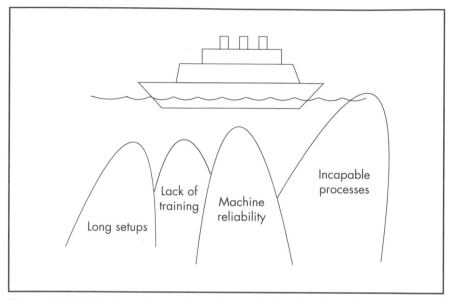

Figure 7-13. Boat, water, and rocks symbolize business, inventory, and problems.

Each rock or problem requires a different solution, and you may not be able to get rid of it immediately. It is okay to navigate around the rock temporarily, but try to avoid covering it back up, or you may never come back to it. Unfortunately, there usually has to be a little pain involved as motivation to get rid of a problem.

If you must select the first choice (raise the water level), write down a date to come back and implement the second choice (remove the rock). Do not forget an opportunity to remove a rock forever. Keep in mind that some tools in the Lean enterprise toolbox are more emotionally charged than others. There is a big impact on personnel as they adjust to reconfigured equipment layouts, implementing pull systems, kanbans, and other very visible techniques. A little caution should be exercised. Any company, especially a job shop, can shoot itself in the foot by racing to these tools before it is ready.

Like a sports team, it is good to be able to make the big play. Whether it is the big pass or the three-point jumpshot, this is what gets attention and brings the crowd to its feet. But to make that big play, a team must be good at the fundamentals—good blocking, dribbling, and passing. Without ball control, you'll never get a chance to move your team down the court to stuff the ball.

A work team has the same need for fundamentals, particularly in the early stages of implementing Lean. There are enough naysayers out there ready to cast stones at the changes you are hoping to make. Don't give them any ammunition. Racing toward a physical layout before you've given adequate attention to the techniques we have talked about is a sure recipe for failure. Let me share an example with you.

At the prompting of a consultant group familiar with implementing the Toyota production system within OEM environments, a company chose to leap over the fundamentals and move right to facilities layout. Perhaps this particular consultant group was unaware of the flexibility necessary in a job shop environment. Whatever the case, they convinced the company that it should reconfigure six separate processes into a cellular configuration. What's wrong with this solution? Nothing, if the fundamentals are managed prior to welding the equipment together. However, this was not the case. Line balancing was only developed for one Takt time. Some setup reduction Kaizens were performed. Standard work and line balancing was attempted. But as soon as the product mix or the volumes changed, the million-dollar realignment became an inefficient behemoth. The layout did not allow staffing the equipment at different levels for different Takt times, nor were people in a position where they could easily help their teammates. This project went wrong because it ignored a basic principle. Two wrongs do not make a right, and two unreliable pieces of equipment bolted together do not make a reliable one.

A secondary problem with the layout was that rather than "right sizing" the equipment, the process was designed using the existing, large, expensive, hard-to-duplicate equipment. So it became a monstrosity that had to serve all possible customers. This created a situation where setup times were enormous and downtime rates were embarrassing. The environment was one in which the team was forced to be "everything to everybody."

Think about this analogy of a family shopping for a new vehicle. As the family members look at all their transportation needs, they determine that, since they need to carry things from time to time, a small car will not work. They have four people in the family, so a standard pickup truck is out of the question. They could buy a club cab for the pickup truck, but they like to go camping. They decide that the best vehicle for them is a 32-ft motor home! They will use it for taking the kids to school, for grocery shopping, getting the mail, and going to church. Sure, it's hard to park, and it uses lots of gas, but after all, everybody fits into it, they can haul things in it, and they will use it once a year for camping.

Of course, the family made a stupid decision. So why do we try to do the same thing with machinery in our shops? We go shopping for or we build a "do-all" or "be-all" machine that becomes a huge, hard to manage, and costly piece of hardware.

Let me back up to the reliability issue. This "everything to everybody" cell was allowed to continue for over three years, until the company ran out of capacity. In exploring the duplication alternatives, it became apparent through a study that the average uptime for this cell was about 53 percent. Once this reliability issue became visible, the pain was unbearable. Did it make sense to duplicate a monster that wasted 47 percent of the day in a setup or breakdown mode? We didn't know why the machine was down so much, so we took digital photographs of each machine center, orientation device, and material-handling mechanism in the process. What surprised us was the sheer number of mechanical devices: 55 distinct mechanical, pneumatic, electronic, or hydraulic devices. This did not include photo cells, limit switches, or similar items.

Laminated copies of the photos were made and they were posted in seven areas throughout the manufacturing line. The operators recorded downtime occurrences and duration to determine the greatest opportunity. The net effect was that by identifying a major reliability problem we came to realize that this company did not need more equipment. They simply needed greater utilization of the equipment they already had.

The company is still working to eliminate the causes of downtime on this machine. The cost of de-linking this cell may be the best short-term solution, until reliability is restored and setups can be managed in under 10 minutes. Fundamentals!

The message is this: these machines should never have been put together in the first place, and the consultant who says "Ready—

Fire—Aim! Solve the problems later!" should think about their irresponsibility.

There is value in the rapid change approach or the "just do it" attitude embodied in the Kaizen (incremental change) approach. Kaizen is all about implementing quick changes. However, Kaikaku (radical change), is a very different approach. Major changes should be considered carefully and only after the fundamentals have been well managed.

Consultants should think long and hard about advising to hastily implement expensive and poorly thought out recommendations. Haste makes waste, and horror stories like this one not only damage the credibility of consultants but also hurt the process of change. People in the shop intuitively know if an idea is half-baked. More importantly, a bad decision can financially cripple a small job shop. Balance, stability, and flexibility must be the watchwords.

Practice the fundamentals before you try to pretend that you are Toyota. Even though practicing the fundamentals is not as satisfying as moving equipment, and may not be what the company wants to hear, consultants need to avoid the potential for long-term damage that can come from applying short-term solutions lacking depth.

Think of a person wanting to get into shape. Nothing he/she can do in one workout session will have any measurable effect. Conversely, a person who eats a triple-decker banana fudge sundae will suffer minimal long-term damage. It is the effort or the neglect applied every day that adds up over time to real change, positive or negative. Practicing before trying to run a marathon, play basketball, or move equipment is a must.

One of the most important considerations is machine reliability. Unless the machines are capable of the quality required or reliable enough to meet the different demand patterns translated into Takt time, don't bolt them together.

To demonstrate how foolish it would be to build such a line when reliability has not been demonstrated, look at Figure 7-14. Imagine 20 pieces of equipment or handling devices all tied together without regard for uptime dependability. Further imagine that we are fortunate enough to have very reliable processes. In fact, two of the machines are 100 percent reliable, and the remaining 18 are each 99 percent reliable.

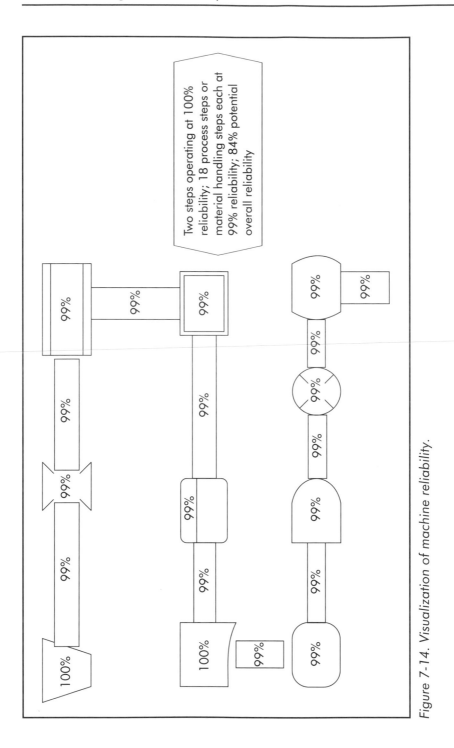

Two steps operating at 100% reliability; 18 process steps or material handling steps each at 99% reliability; 84% potential overall reliability

Figure 7-14. Visualization of machine reliability.

If all the stars and moons line up we may never have any down-time, but what is the potential for uptime problems? If you multiply 99 percent times 99 percent eighteen times, you will eventually get 84 percent. Who wants to live with 84 percent potential reliability? Yet, this is the risk of jumping to extremes before getting good at the fundamentals. To put this into perspective, here is an example of how easily lulled to sleep we are in terms of ensuring machine reliability, and the negative effect that neglect can have on productivity.

Years ago, I bought a used car. After I bought it, little mechanical and electrical problems started to develop. One I particularly remember was an oil leak from the oil-pressure sending unit. It was tucked up underneath the exhaust manifold, and I could never get a wrench in to tighten it up. So, it dripped ever so slightly onto one of the exhaust pipes. I wouldn't notice it as I drove merrily along the freeway, but every time I pulled up to a stop light, an indiscernible puff of smoke would seep out from the seams around the hood. It was obvious to me, but other drivers sharing the stoplight with me weren't able to see the smoke. But, they were able to smell it if their windows were open. My guess is that they all checked their engines when they got home.

There was also an electrical problem that randomly occurred. Every week or so, when I could least afford the time, the car would not start. It was as if there was no battery in the car. No dashboard lights, no starter turning over, no radio, nothing. Then two, five, 10 minutes later, it would start whether or not I opened the hood to wiggle all the wires around. This seven-year-old car also had a few other problems, including the passenger side window that would not roll down. The gear had evidently been stripped and you could push and pull the window up or down by hand, but it was a nuisance. The defroster worked, but you couldn't shut it off. This was not a problem in the winter, but in the summer, the temperature inside the little car was close to that of the surface of the sun.

The point is this: I would never have purchased this car if all these conditions had existed to begin with, so why did I live with it for so long? The real cause of my problem was familiarity and overlooking individual minor problems that collectively added up to major issues. I do not have exclusive rights to this story. One of the engineers in our company described a similar set of mechanical faults with a little car that he was getting ready to sell.

The phenomenon of overlooking the faults of things familiar can be a good thing if you are talking about people. Patience with the shortcomings and faults of friends and family members is an admirable trait. But, when dealing with machine reliability in plants, overlooking a growing list of faults can cost a great deal.

If we were to go shopping for a new piece of equipment, ready to spend hundreds of thousands of dollars on a new machine, would we accept a 50, 60, 70 percent reliability rate? No, we would turn on our heel and head for the door. Yet, we allow the existing machinery in our plants to become like my old car. A little less reliable every day, one more idiosyncrasy, until we wake up one morning and realize what we have is an unreliable, labor-intensive bottleneck that must be nursed every step of the way. To avoid this scenario, we must ensure that there is a total productive maintenance (TPM) program in place, especially before the transition from departmental layout to cellular layout.

JIDOKA AND POKA-YOKE

Closely related to machine reliability is jidoka and poka-yoke. Roughly translated, *jidoka* means that there is a device to ensure that the machine is producing good parts all the time. In case something falls out of the bed, the machine is smart enough to stop itself or notify the operator. *Poka-yoke* is, for a lack of a better term, "Murphy-proofing" (my apologies to everybody named Murphy). Remember Murphy's law? It says that if anything can go wrong, it will. Poka-yoke devices are built to challenge Murphy's law. A better term for poka-yoke might be "mistake-proofing." This requires building a mechanism or a process that cannot produce any defects or more than one fault.

Jidoka implies autonomation. Not automation, but autonomation, meaning self-governing. The machine is able to recognize when a fault has occurred and stop itself or notify someone of the problem. A good example of this is in the sheet metal industry. Some stand-alone turret punches run "lights out," that is, they run at night, alone. If the machine misloads a sheet of material, a sensor detects the misalignment and stops. A phone call is placed by the machine to the operator's pager or even to his/her home phone. The operator can then come to the machine to fix the error. You would not want this happening every night. But, it does allow the operator to leave the machine to do more operator-intensive things rather than having to wait by the machine for a defect or fault that may never happen.

A simple and common example of a poka-yoke device is built into every videotape cassette player: you cannot load the videotape backwards or upside down. If you try, the machine will kick it back out. The same basic principle is used with computer disks. Another example is leaded versus unleaded gasoline pump nozzles. When the change from leaded to unleaded gasoline was made, the car manufacturers designed the receivers in the car to accept only spouts for unleaded gas. It made it nearly impossible to put leaded gas into a car designed to burn unleaded gas. The nozzle will simply not fit. They poka-yoke'd the entire process.

The process of designing jidoka and poka-yoke devices should not rest solely with the engineering department. Some engineers have a tendency to over-engineer such things. You then need a device to check the device. Operators will often suggest simpler and more effective devices.

Jidoka and poka-yoke devices can be expensive, but a product- or process-generic design can reap multiple benefits. In the long run these devices can pay nice dividends. If and when you can give jidoka and poka-yoke a try, you will be surprised at the ideas that come out of a Kaizen event of this type.

PULL SYSTEMS

If I have the story right, it was one of the managers from Toyota on a visit to the United States in the late 1960s or early 1970s who noticed that American mini-markets used a unique method of stocking the shelves. I don't know exactly how the story developed, but allow me to take editorial license with it.

Imagine a small mini-market. A Japanese visitor observed the people coming and going. One customer retrieved a loaf of bread. The next grabbed a bag of chips and a soda. The following person purchased some cookies and milk. The visitor walked over to the cooler and quickly calculated that it could hold perhaps 700 cans

115

of soft drinks and beer. The baked goods shelves were stocked with no more than 25 loaves of bread. The potato chips were stored in a small cardboard display roughly the size of a curio cabinet. How could the store hope to stay in business? Our Japanese friend approached the store manager and asked, "Where do you keep all the stock? So many people are coming and going; you will be out of everything in two days." The manager explained that if the visitor were to come back in the morning between 5:00 and 7:00 a.m., he would see the potato chip delivery van pull up and restock the shelves with just what had been consumed the previous day. The same thing would happen with the dairy, the bakery, and the soda deliveries. If no sodas were sold, then none would be stocked. That truck driver would simply drive on to the next stop.

Exploring the rest of this food chain, the Japanese visitor discovered that the delivery truck also had to be loaded every day, replenishing what was delivered to the stores. This required a stock location at a warehouse or distribution center. When the warehouse shelf got to a certain level, then the warehouse workers had a signal to send more material. If no signal came, they knew the shelf was stocked. In a nutshell, this is an example and definition of pull: customer demand translated into a signal to move or manufacture product. The material is demanded or pulled rather than being forced or pushed though the system.

The process evidently made a great deal of sense to the visitor. When he applied it to the manufacturing processes back at Toyota, this very American solution to servicing the needs of the customer became the undoing of traditional batch manufacturing in Japan. It also marked the beginning of the end for some American car companies who were unable or unwilling to change their manufacturing processes to a model process developed in their own backyard. Nevertheless, their Japanese manufacturing counterparts successfully adapted and used it in an entirely new way.

Having a mini-market of some stock items certainly is a logical approach when you are making cars or trucks, since they all use brake pads, brake pedals, and brake fluid. Having some of each of these delivered just as they are consumed, just when they are required, and just in the right quantities makes perfect sense, right? While this may be the best approach in an assembly process, or even in a moderate- to high-volume mass-production process, wouldn't this be a very expensive way for a job shop to operate? Good questions, and well worth exploring. Stocking a few of every item could get to be expensive for a job shop that may have 1,000, 2,000, or 3,000 potential part numbers.

The best economic solution might again be a hybrid approach. If you performed the Product Quantity Routing (PQR) analysis described earlier, you can use this data to assist in determining the best candidates for setting up pull systems. It is important to recognize that not all products lend themselves to use of the pull system. Table 7-10 (also shown earlier as Table 5-3) shows criteria used by one company to select the best candidates for use in a pull system. In this example, the teams operating the Just-in-Time (JIT) cells focused on highly repetitive parts, pulling material from a finished goods location and replenishing the consumption from a work-in-process (WIP) mini-market. When the WIP was depleted to a predetermined level, the manufacturing process was signaled to make more. This is very much like the system observed at the mini-market by the Japanese visitor.

As a visual tool, notice how Figure 7-15 graphically shows how a hybrid approach might work in a manufacturing environment such as Stan and Fran's Jobbe Shoppe. Pay particular attention to the curved arrows. These symbolize a physical pull or move of material. These pulls happen only if a product has been consumed. I refer to this as a hybrid approach because it is neither a true pull system nor is it a true batch system. It is somewhere in the middle. It allows the flexibility necessary in a job shop, yet allows quicker response than a traditional batch-push model.

In the previous example, the truck driver only leaves material if there is an empty spot available for it at the customer's point of use. He/she restocks the truck only if the need exists. The assembly function builds a unit only if the driver has removed one. The fabrication process is triggered to manufacture a lot size only if the assembly WIP falls below a predetermined level.

One of the greatest challenges facing job shops is the often irregular ordering pattern of customers. Sometimes customers who have the same equipment or manufacturing capabilities as their suppliers use the vendor as a pressure-relief valve from demand spikes in their own order file. The mom-and-pop shop ends up

Table 7-10. Hybrid plant layout concept

Special Cells 15% Sales	Standard Cells 25% Sales	Just-in-time (JIT) Cells 60% Sales
Prototypes	Proven CNC programs	All the conditions of the standard cell product plus:
Untested CNC programs	Parts that will run again	Customer forecasts fairly accurate
One-of-a-kind special tooling	Setups documented	Customers buy into just-in-time (JIT) programs
Engineered to order	Quality requirements defined	Vendors support the required lead times

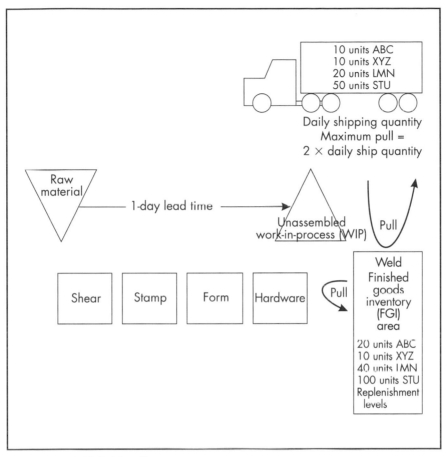

Figure 7-15. Hybrid pull system.

getting orders only when the customers have too little capacity themselves, and jobs "fall off the plate," so to speak. This can cause unforeseen and hard-to-manage spikes in the supplier organization.

It is unreasonable to imagine that spikes can ever be predicted with infallible accuracy, or that they will ever completely go away. If you can smooth them out by using a supermarket of material, it can help act as a shock-absorbing device. This will allow you to more easily meet even the difficult demands of the customer. This works especially well for material that can be used for more than one item.

Being able to replenish a WIP of finished goods inventory area at your convenience rather than at the drop of a hat makes it possible to manufacture something else at the drop of a hat.

For processes that cannot be tied directly together, there is one more tool we need to talk about—standard WIP. Almost every consultant will tell you that the goal of Lean is to avoid inventory in all its forms, and most of the time that is true. However, there are situations that can warrant a small buffer of material. For example, there may be two processes that cannot be hard linked or a major imbalance in setup or process times. A small quantity or queue of material can help cushion against surges until you can perfect the flow. We call this queue of material *standard WIP*. It should be kept to a minimum and there should be devices (systems) in place to physically limit the amount.

If we take a second look at the mini-market analogy, remember there were about 25 loaves of bread. The bakery truck did not deliver a loaf every time one was taken. This is the principle we need to think about in designing a pull system using standard WIP: determine the minimum amount of material between each station and never allow it to grow beyond that level.

We should not rely solely on the memory of people to manage what might be dozens of standard WIP locations. We may end up with unhappy customers (internal or external). If the bakery left it to chance that the truck driver would stop and look at the shelf at every store, it would have unhappy customers. A more reliable system might be to use a barcode signal from the store to the warehouse and from the warehouse to the bakery. Most companies applying pull systems have found that a physical signal to replenish the standard WIP works well to avoid stock-out issues or overproduction.

A famous American motorcycle manufacturer has refined a process referred to as a "two bin" system. Simple and somewhat self-managing, each operator has two or more bins or totes from which they work. This is their standard WIP. When one of the bins is empty, the operator sets it to the back and begins using the remaining bin(s). On a regular schedule, a tractor driver pulling a little train of carts moves up and down every aisle collecting empty bins.

Each bin might have a unique card inside that describes the part. Information may be attached directly to the bin regarding where the bin is coming from and where it is going. The card also might define lot size, the quality requirements, part specifications, references to blueprint numbers or setup sheets, and information regarding the required replenishment time (turnaround time). All of this information can be defined within or directly on the bin itself. You can see how easily this could cut down on paperwork.

The size of the bin is determined by how long it takes to replenish it and how fast the parts are consumed. If the machine shop can turn out 10 cam shafts in an hour and the person assembling engines needs 100 shafts per day, then each bin may hold at least two hours worth of material. This will ensure that the operator will never run dry.

The same system can be used with cards instead of bins, or barcodes instead of cards, or flashing lights instead of barcodes. Whatever the signal, it must trigger before the operator actually runs out, and the signal must turn off once the replenishment cycle has begun.

Figure 7-16 is similar to Figure 7-15, but there is a new symbol between each process. This symbol is the amount of units allowed between each process. If the operator fills the standard WIP and the next process has not pulled the material, then this time can be used to help flush out the system, perform preventive maintenance, do housekeeping, or cross-train.

As soon as the standard WIP is consumed, the operator can return to producing to Takt time. If an operator begins to recognize a pattern that requires him/her to stop more often than usual, then this may indicate that the standard work is not balanced and may need to be adjusted.

Holding finished goods and standard WIP for material that is not forecast well or runs infrequently can be a risky endeavor. If you cannot get good information from the buyer, find another indicator, if possible. One company could not get good forecasting information from the customer's sheet metal buyer. They found the supplier for the customer's circuit boards and, by sharing information with the planner at that manufacturer, were able to obtain additional information that helped each supplier make better

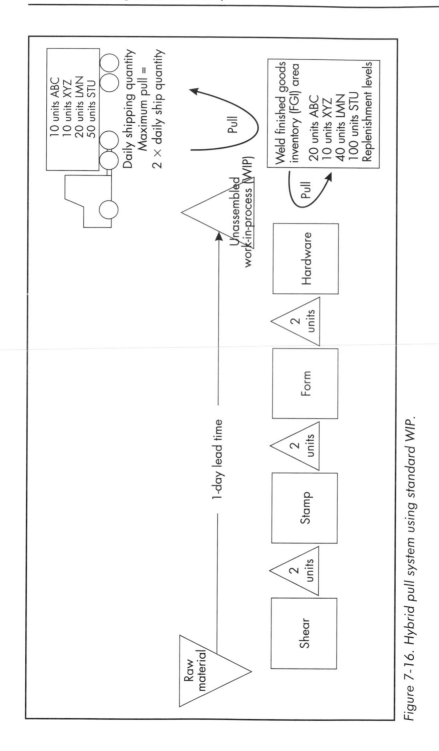

Figure 7-16. Hybrid pull system using standard WIP.

forecasting decisions. The lead time on circuit boards was four or five times the lead time for sheet metal, and the forecasts provided to the board manufacturer were always much closer to reality than those provided to the sheet metal supplier.

Get creative and find the indicators that allow you to smooth your production plan. You may need to become a bit of a detective.

FACILITIES PLANNING

Laying out an entire plant can be a very time-consuming process. The challenges associated with rearranging the machines inside a plant that has grown into a departmental mammoth can be more difficult than starting from scratch. It begins to resemble a chess game. "First we have to move this, not because we have a place for it yet, but just to get it out of the way so that we can move that. Then, we can clear a space for the first thing we moved."

There are many tools available for planning an entire facility layout and they can be complicated without advanced training. To visualize the possible number of steps necessary, look at Figure 7-17. It shows a flow chart with each step identified in a suggested order of execution. The section following the flow chart defines some of the more critical steps in the facility planning process.

Having knowledge of the tools does not mean you can go out and begin laying out an entire facility. But, they can guide you and an engineering team through the process. Explaining all the details, options, and alternatives to this process would double the size of this book. This is an area where you need the assistance of an expert. However, an expert industrial engineer may not understand the Lean approach, so an explanation of your goals may be necessary.

The steps needed for facility planning are given in Figure 7-18.

One of the best ways to determine the best possible layout for a cell or a plant is to know the relative importance of one activity to another. Then, place the activities in their new location based on their importance of being there. You can rank the relative importance of proximity between one operation or activity and another. Assign a number value from 0 to 5:

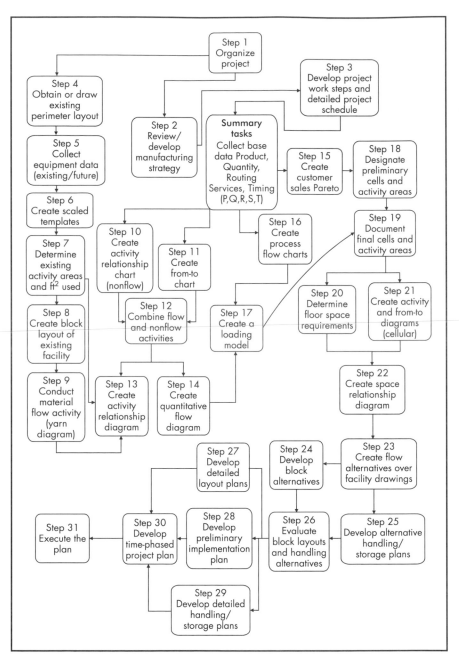

Figure 7-17. Facility planning steps in suggested order of execution.

0 = Undesirable
1 = Not important
2 = Preferred
3 = Important
4 = Extremely important
5 = Critical

Table 7-11 shows a blank relationship matrix. Table 7-12 shows how it looks filled in, and conceptually the importance of the relationships. All the operations, activities, and storage locations need to be listed. Ask the same question for each: how important is the physical proximity of the shear to the punch? How important is the physical proximity of the shear to the forming station? How important is the physical proximity of the shear to the deburr station? And so forth. Rate your answers using the scale of 0-5 just described.

If there is a reason for two operations to be at a distance, either for environmental or safety reasons, score these at zero. For example, notice that weld and wash rates a zero, even though the flow of material is generally from weld to wash. This is a phosphate wash system and welding fumes mixed with the chemicals in the washing system can be harmful under certain conditions, so these two activities should not be within close proximity.

Once the operations or activities have been ranked, build a visual representation that shows the relative importance between them (see Figure 7-19). Connect each activity area to all other activity areas with the same number of lines as the value assigned in Table 7-12. For example, the punch and wash activities have only two lines connecting them, but the punch and deburr operations would have four lines connecting them.

Think about the lines like rubber bands: the more rubber bands connecting two operations or activities, the more pull one can exert on the other. The fewer the rubber bands, the less influence they can exert.

The next step is to define the square footage required for each activity, operation, or storage area. Develop a block layout, which doesn't need to have all the fine details, but begins to allow material flow patterns to be brainstormed.

Facility Planning Checklist

1. Organize the project (executive team)
   ___ Objectives identified
   ___ Scope defined
   ___ Steering team identified
   ___ Project team identified
   ___ Project documentation log/file setup
   ___ Project work steps and dates available
2. Review/develop manufacturing strategy (executive team)
   ___ Constraints identified
   ___ Assumptions identified
   ___ Maximum capacity/volumes identified
   ___ Alternative technology identified
3. Collect base data Product, Quantity, Routing, Support Systems, Time (PQRST) (sales/process routings/product catalogs/production schedules)
   ___ Process charts
   ___ Product I.D.
   ___ Capacity spreadsheet
   ___ Sales volume (PQR)
   ___ Timing parameters
   ___ Equipment data sheets
   ___ Inventory
   ___ Working patterns (shift schedules)
   ___ Activity area sheet (Muther method)
   ___ Machinery data work sheet (Muther method)
4. Identify Just-in-Time (JIT) product families/activity areas (plant layout drawings/ equipment list)
   ___ Activity areas identified and numbered
   ___ Products grouped for cell design
   ___ Equipment to product mix identified
   ___ Machines/tooling compatible with products
   ___ Develop "rough cut" cell loading spreadsheet
5. Analyze material, information, and inventory flow
   ___ Value stream map
   ___ Map information flow
   ___ Identify inventory flow patterns
   ___ Analyze nonflow relationships
6. Develop relationship diagram (relationship chart)
   ___ Code and identify all relationships
   ___ Rate importance of activity center relationships
7. Determine space availability (strategy document/plant layout drawings)
   ___ Determine necessary work-in-process (WIP) space requirements
   ___ Outsource products/parts identified
   ___ Outsource processes identified
   ___ Parking requirements identified

Figure 7-18. Facility planning checklist.

8. Calculate space requirements (plant layout/machine templates)
   ___ Size equipment
   ___ Determine area needed for machines and WIP
   ___ Aisle space
   ___ Machine repair accessibility
   ___ Material handling area
   ___ Area for scrap, boxes, etc.
   ___ Rough detail (air, power, utility requirements)

9. Calculate future space requirements (manufacturing strategy/maximum capacity/volume spreadsheet)
   ___ Identify new technologies under consideration
   ___ Outsourced processes being brought in house
   ___ Facility requirements at full capacity
   ___ Parking and office at full capacity

10. Develop space relationship diagram (relationship diagram)
    ___ Develop area blocks (work area)

11. Develop block layout alternatives (relationship diagrams/area blocks)
    ___ Identify material flow routes
    ___ Identify alternate shipping/receiving points
    ___ Ensure that all activity areas and process relationships are honored
    ___ Consider noise, dirt, etc., conditions
    ___ Consider constraint conditions

12. Develop alternate handling/storage plans (material handling checklist)
    ___ Raw-in-process (RIP) system identified
    ___ Kanban pull system identified
    ___ Handling equipment/technologies identified

13. Evaluate layout and handling alternatives (block layout alternatives)
    ___ Identify unique features of each alternative
    ___ Straw-man factors and considerations on form
    ___ Score each alternative
    ___ Block alternative evaluation (Muther method)

14. Develop detailed layout plans, handling/storage ("winning block" alternative/material handing)
    ___ Simulate operations
    ___ Project team/steering team buy-in
    ___ Cost figures
    ___ Final printed or electronic templates

15. Present final layout and handling plans (detailed layout/project documentation book)
    ___ Approval by executive team
    ___ Update all drawings and data in project book

Figure 7-18. (continued).

Table 7-11. Blank relationship matrix

	Raw material storage	Shear	Punch	Deburr	Form	Weld	Wash	Paint	Paint storage	Packaging	Shipping/receiving	Restrooms
Raw material storage												
Shear												
Punch												
Deburr												
Form												
Weld												
Wash												
Paint												
Paint storage												
Packaging												
Shipping/receiving												
Restrooms												

As you can see, there are a number of steps required to logically and effectively set up a cell. Laying out an entire plant is simply repeating this exercise for each value stream. Before you know it, you have a facility layout.

There are several good books on the subject of facility planning. The approach may not completely apply to the Lean approach or cellular layout, but the thought process works well for designing each cell. If, after you have identified the needs of each cell, you look at each cell as an individual machine, then the process can work fairly well for an entire plant.

Back to the Jobbe Shoppe

Let's go back and listen in as Jan, Stan, and the rest of the team discuss how to layout their model line.

Table 7-12. Completed relationship matrix

	Raw material storage	Shear	Punch	Deburr	Form	Weld	Wash	Paint	Paint storage	Packaging	Shipping/receiving	Restrooms
Raw material storage		4	3	2	1	1	0	0	0	0	4	2
Shear			4	3	2	2	1	1	0	1	1	2
Punch				4	4	3	2	2	0	2	2	2
Deburr					4	3	3	2	0	2	2	2
Form						4	3	2	0	3	2	2
Weld							0	3	0	2	1	2
Wash								4	5	3	2	2
Paint									5	4	3	2
Paint storage										0	2	2
Packaging											5	2
Shipping/receiving												2
Restrooms												

It is 6:00 a.m. Thursday morning and the team has spent three days organizing all the data, performing time studies, calculating Takt times and standard work, and designing a system to pull material through the welding cell.

Stan is standing next to a wall covered with notes, remnants of their work to develop standard work for the team. He raises a point that has been on everyone's mind. "Jan, we have calculated the ideal crew size and we know the Takt time at each of three sales levels. We have the standard work defined and we now know how to pull material through the shop using kanban signals, but I'll bet there is no mathematical formula to calculate the best machine layout."

Jan nods, amused, and replies, "I knew this was coming, but I have to commend the team for holding back this long. Most companies want to jump ahead, skip over the fundamentals, and go

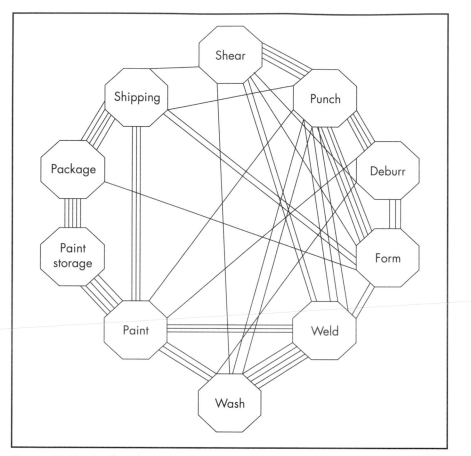

Figure 7-19. Spider diagram showing the relative importance between all operations and activities.

right to moving equipment. I think you have to admit that we know a lot more about the process than we did four days ago. Therefore, we now know a lot more about how to lay out our cell than we did when we started.

"Today is the day we should begin thinking about the layout. We need to decide if we will use a virtual or physical cell. We won't move any equipment today, but by using our future state map, we can begin the process of developing a detailed layout."

Leanne asks a question for everybody. "What do you mean by *virtual cell*?"

Jan apologizes for using an unfamiliar term, and then explains. "Sometimes there are reasons why we can't physically move the equipment right away. So instead of losing the benefits of all the planning, some companies decide to implement as much of the program as they can until they can remove whatever the barriers are, or until the barriers become less important. Most teams operating in a virtual cell are the driving force behind a company finally moving the equipment, because it often creates problems for the team to be at a distance from each other. Communication suffers, and it is definitely more difficult to operate as a team, to share work, help on setups, and so forth. The team usually drives the management team to move the equipment closer together or to obtain right-sized equipment, so they no longer have to be at a distance or viewed as a shared resource.

"A virtual cell is usually a last option. It is a management decision whether or not we move the machinery right away, but the layout itself is something we need to do now. The plan will be complete regardless of when we begin scooting equipment around, or when the riggers are finally called in."

Everyone casts a sideways glance at Stan, hoping to get an indication of whether the move will happen sooner or later. Jan smiles and relieves the tension by wagging his head and saying "Okay, first let's get this layout done and then we should know what it will take to make it happen. The first thing we need to do is identify the machine capabilities needed for this product line and any potential product we expect to join the work flowing through this cell."

The team develops a machine specification list, keeping in mind the need for each piece of equipment to meet the Takt time. They then compare the remaining equipment list with parts that need to run through the rest of the shop, but not through the cell. They do this to ensure that the remaining machines in the shop will have all the capabilities they need without needing to borrow the cell equipment. It is all right to violate this occasionally, but if there are constant interruptions, the cell will never be able to work effectively as a unit.

Jan pulls out a checklist of information the team needs to gather, along with issues that it needs to think about and organize in preparation for developing what he calls a "block layout." The list looks like this:

- Machine list;
- Machine footprint (machine sizes including traversing movement);
- Machine repair/maintenance accessibility areas;
- Material handling areas;
- Areas for scrap, boxes, etc.;
- Power, air, hydraulic, utility requirements;
- Noise, dirt, special considerations;
- Material handling equipment access;
- Blueprints of the area;
- Scissors;
- Paper outlines of the machines, tables, skate tracks, etc., to be used; and
- Clear tape or pins.

A *block layout* is simply a "rough-cut" area location and material flow example. It shows the square footage utilized by the cell and all the surrounding equipment. This is done in abstract. Hand-drawn sketches are fine for this process. The drawings will be used by the team to study concepts for feasibility before developing a detailed layout. If you can rule out an idea before going to the detail layout stage, a lot of time can be saved. Try to come up with at least seven alternative block layouts to select from. We will discuss how to narrow down and select the best layout in the section on total quality management.

One of the questions that will ultimately arise is whether to hard link or soft link two pieces of equipment. In an OEM environment, hard linking makes a lot of sense. In a job shop, it depends on the percentage of time material flows uninterrupted through all the machines under consideration.

If studies show that material *deadheads* (material runs through one of the machines but nothing happens to it) a significant percentage of the time, question seriously whether they should be linked. Also, if deadheading the material through one of the machines requires significant setup time, avoid it.

Figures 7-20 and 7-21 show examples of potential material flow through a shop using five distinct cells. Each cell would need to be laid out individually. Try to develop seven or more alternative flow patterns. Of course, these figures are conceptual only. The

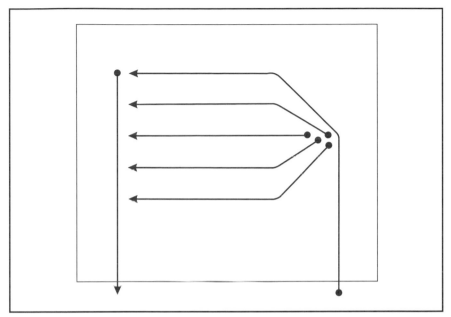

Figure 7-20. Abstract material flow diagram (version 1).

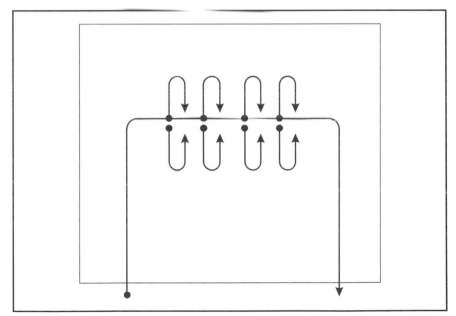

Figure 7-21. Abstract material flow diagram (version 2).

actual footprint of each machine needs to be defined, developed into a block layout, and then into a detailed layout. Attention must be given to items such as those in the following list (there may be additional issues as well) as the block and detail layouts are developed:

- Raw material flow;
- Finished material flow;
- Standard WIP;
- Forklift, pallet jack, or cart access;
- Machine repair;
- Crew movements (at different Takt times); and
- Machine movements (X-Y-Z coordinate movements).

MATERIAL HANDLING REDUCTION

Material handling, usually one of the greatest opportunities to remove non-value-added labor, is a difficult subject. There are no formulas or scientific solutions to avoid excess handling. The challenge is to keep operators working. Until the facility is laid out so that material flows with little or no additional personnel, you may need to apply a stop-gap measure to prevent operators from moving material.

The Japanese have a word, *mish-u-shu-mashi,* which roughly translates to "water spider," a small creature that skips across the water. Like water spiders, some team members move quickly around the cell to assist in whatever needs to be done to keep the material moving or flowing. These team members may not have a distinct production job title or function, but they provide break relief, assist in setup preparation, help perform external activities, and so forth. Their duties need to be defined, but not to the level of detail that the cycle time work steps need definition.

Not every value stream or model line needs a water spider. This person is often a temporary or interim fix employed only if there are significant setup issues, excessive distances between operations, and material handling issues. Because this person serves as an information conduit, he/she needs to have strong communication skills, enthusiasm, energy, a helpful nature, and a positive attitude. Careful consideration should be given to the selection of this team member.

SUMMARY

Each of the ten techniques discussed in this chapter are critical to companies of every size. Practice these fundamentals well. Use them first in a model line, then apply them throughout your entire facility.

Managing Change

The change to the Lean approach is fueled by people. Regardless of how well your shop is designed or how accurate the Takt Time calculations are, without the best efforts of people, the benefits will be small and slow in coming. No amount of supervision or directive ability will prove effective if the folks asked to operate in this new environment are unaware of the need for, or unwilling to offer, their participation.

The technical aspects of the Lean approach described so far in this book are what I call "hard skills." But there is a separate set of skills necessary when you must approach co-workers and subordinates and encourage them to be co-implementers of these techniques. Without the right set of tools, this approach can be challenging, intimidating, and stressful for all parties involved. It will be nearly impossible to fully turn your operation into one that focuses on value-added rather than non-value-added activities without the support of others.

The tool kit you need in this transition will not be found in the hard skills of Lean, Total Quality Management (TQM), or Just-in-Time (JIT). The techniques required here are a package of "soft skills."

We are asking people to change, to lose the "ham bone mentality," and to adapt to a method that must at first seem to fly in the face of reason. Put yourself in the place of an operator. Performing the setup has always been the fun part of the day. This is generally the only time an operator can be creative and take a break from the mind-numbing job of feeding parts into a machine. Now, we are asking him/her to think of setup not as a friend, but as an enemy, something to avoid. Change is hard, and without an accurate understanding of why, there can be no commitment to make it work.

Three phrases summarize how people in the manufacturing environment learn. The phrases are:

- Tell me, and I forget.
- Show me, and I remember.
- Involve me, and I understand.

Leaders who understand the power of these simple phrases and apply them to change will recognize a greater measure of success. Leaders who choose to ignore the fundamental principles embodied in these phrases, who hurry past the message, or who fail to realize these words relate to basic human emotional needs, will read right past them as if they were mere ink on a page. Then three, four, or five years later, these same managers will be frustrated that their efforts to implement Lean have not worked. They will be the greatest critics of the process and they will blame their failure on the economic climate, the lack of capable employees, or the differences between the American and Japanese cultures. They will say things like, "It worked in Japan because that's how people were raised. It doesn't work here in America, I tried it!"

Attention to the human need for true involvement is more important than is usually known. Determining how people feel is usually outside the typical metrics used by chief executive officers (CEOs) and chief financial officers (CFOs) to measure a company's performance or a manager's skill.

I saw a bumper sticker on a car that said: "Advice from a wing walker: Don't let go with one hand until you get a firm grip with the other." When the wing walker needs to move, it must be done carefully and with the new grip completely solid before turning the former handhold loose. If someone were pushing him or hurrying him through the process, the risk of losing him off the wing would increase greatly. What the message meant to me was that for years we have asked people to do things a certain way, like a wing walker holding onto a bar on the wing of an airplane.

By involving people in change and allowing them the time and chance to make the transition at a reasonable rate rather than yelling them through it, they and the company stand a much higher chance of successfully moving from point to point.

There are entire books devoted to helping leaders and companies become more effective agents of change. I cannot summarize in this text the information that has been given about human nature and the need to meet the personal and practical needs of people. However, I can share with you five critical needs, and the negative effect of ignoring any one of them as change is being introduced.

NEEDS OF THE PEOPLE

The five critical needs are: vision, skills, incentive (or WIIFM: what's in it for me?), resources, and an action plan.

Vision

Providing a vision seems so logical that you wouldn't think it needs to be discussed. But it is amazing how little effort goes into developing a clear and communicated concept of what the company should look like. In the second row from the top in Figure 8-1, notice how neglecting the critical need for a vision will not lead to change, but will instead result in confusion.

Just as a football team needs to know which end of the field they will be running toward, people need to see the figurative goalpost to understand where to apply their efforts and to drive toward it. Having clearly defined goals also helps to remove projects that do not support the vision.

Skills

Skills training is another critical need. Even though a football team may understand which end of the field is theirs, they need to know how to operate as a team, and this takes training. Providing the teams with training in how to develop and use standard work, setup reduction, and the other tools is key if they are to share in implementing change. Otherwise, as Figure 8-1 shows, the result will be anxiety rather than effective change (more about this later).

Incentives

"What's in it for me?" This does not always mean financial incentives. People require basic human interaction and contact, and one of the greatest incentives is attention. Taking the time to

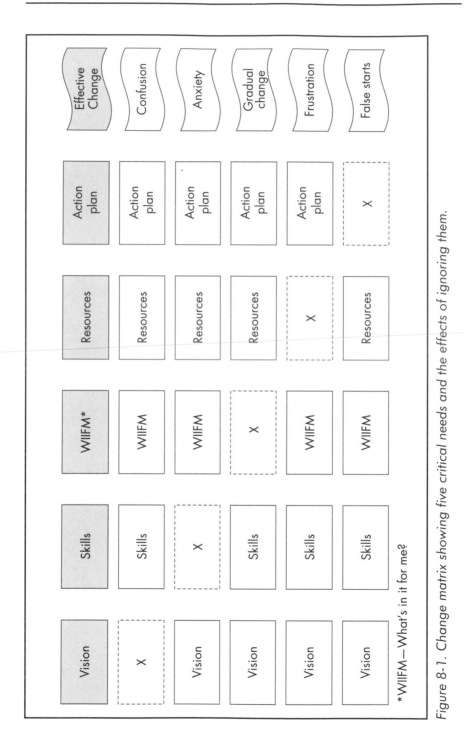

*WIIFM—What's in it for me?

Figure 8-1. Change matrix showing five critical needs and the effects of ignoring them.

acknowledge effort, recognize accomplishment, and offer feedback (either positive or corrective) can be one of the most powerful forms of this key element. Without it, the change will be gradual.

At some point into the Lean transformation, usually two to three years, financial incentive programs might make sense, but don't race to this. Much like the discussion of physical plant layout, where moving equipment too early can sometimes have the effect of "shooting yourself in the foot," putting an incentive program in place too early can be counter-productive. The planning, manufacturing, and quality systems must be stable before moving toward a financial incentive program. We will talk more about gain-sharing in a later chapter.

Resources

Another key element in change management is resources. Asking for change, but not allowing time or providing opportunity to participate, can lead teams and individuals away from change and toward frustration. They may see the vision and even be trained to carry it out. They may understand the rewards for themselves. But if they can't get it done because of a lack of funding or time or whatever, they will walk away with their hands in the air. Resource planning for the Lean approach simply needs to be a part of the regular budgeting process. If you fail to plan, plan to fail.

Planning

The last key element in change management is the action plan. When a football team takes the field, they shouldn't wonder about the first few plays. They should have an action plan. If you pull any team members aside, they should be able to tell you the next play. They may not need to know which plays will be run in the fourth quarter. Time and events during the game will force adjustment to the long range plan, and that's all right. The team just needs to know the next few plays clearly. The same is true for work teams. A basic plan of action should not be left to chance and each member should be able to describe the next few steps. A time-phased project plan can be used to help educate the team in their short-term goals.

Table 8-1 shows a simple chart or time-phased project plan. We will discuss this tool in greater detail in Chapter 14. Without a clear plan of action, you can imagine the result. As Figure 8-1 shows, the outcome will be chaos and false starts.

Table 8-1. Example of time-phased project plan

Activity	Assigned to	1	2	3	4	5	6
Perform product-quantity-routing (PQR) analysis	Stan/Jan	X					
Measure operator cycle time	Team		X				
Calculate Takt times	Team			X			
Develop standard work	Leanne, Fran			X			

Quality System Management: Tools for the Team

An illustration in Chapter Two, Figure 2-2, showed a wheel that pictured how the key business principles related to quality. The spokes on this wheel symbolize a few critical indicators used to measure how well a company has addressed the quality aspect of doing business.

You may think of other spokes to add, such as the quality system known as "six-sigma." Or, you may feel that some of the subjects included here 5-S: sort, straighten, shine, standardize, and sustain (organizational house keeping), and *Poka-yoke* (mistake proofing) belong only in the Lean techniques section rather than in the chapter dedicated to quality. How you approach the measurement is totally up to you. This is only a mental model. The important point is: whatever gets measured, gets improved.

TOTAL QUALITY MANAGEMENT

The tools within the Total Quality Management (TQM) toolbox are many and varied. One book lists over 700 tools teams can use to navigate through the maze of problems that crop up over time. The goal of this book is to show how a few such tools can make the implementation process faster and easier (see Figure 9-1).

Besides the observation sheets and spaghetti diagram in the discussion of setup reduction, and in addition to the Value Stream Mapping[SM] tools described earlier, there are seven primary tools used on a fairly routine basis. This chapter will discuss each tool and provide explanations and examples of how you and your team might use them. The tools are:

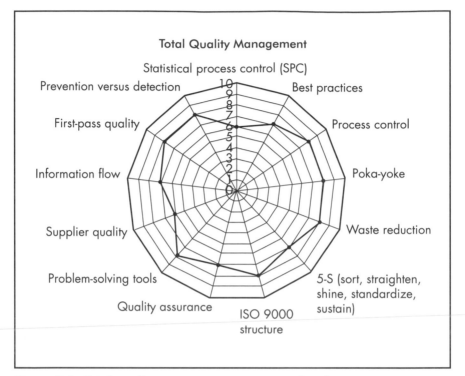

Figure 9-1. Total quality system management radar chart.

- Linearity charts (productivity and waste),
- Ishikawa diagrams (cause-and-effect),
- Quality maps,
- Process flow diagrams,
- Deployment flow charts,
- Pareto analyses, and
- Alternative selection worksheets.

Linearity Charts (Productivity and Waste)

As shown in Chapter 6 (Figures 6-2 and 6-3), linearity charts can be used by the team to monitor progress during the day. This same tool can be used to monitor productivity against planned goals. Waste can also be measured. This is important if there is a built-in waste percentage in the process (that is, machining, molding, or defect removal, saw kerf, etc.).

Ishikawa Diagrams (Cause-and-effect)

The Ishikawa diagram is also referred to as the cause-and-effect diagram because it attempts to assign potential causes to any effect being examined. It is easy to see how the shape of the tool led to its nickname, the "fishbone" diagram. Figure 9-2 shows an example of an Ishikawa diagram.

The six causes generally assigned to the Ishikawa diagram are machines, labor, management (policy or information), materials, method, and Mother Nature (the environment). The process is a bit like peeling an onion. The goal is to get to the core or root cause of the problem or effect. Branches from one or more potential causes can help lead you to the real culprit. This tool is useful not only for solving quality-related problems, but for productivity, delivery, lead time, setup, safety, or morale issues as well.

A problem is not solved just because you identify it. Another brainstorming session and a different set of problem-solving tools are often needed to help you permanently resolve the problem.

Quality Maps

Similar in purpose but different in approach, the quality mapping process is very much like the Value Stream Mapping process, but focuses the attention primarily on key quality issues. The process works like this: get an instant film or digital camera and take pictures of every single activity in the process, regardless of how insignificant it may be. Then, attach the photos (in proper sequence) across the top of a chart (or wall). Underneath each photograph, describe the process in the photo. Figure 9-3 shows an example of a quality map.

Have the team work through every step of the process, from the customer backward to the raw material, answering each of the six questions for each process. Before you know it, you will have a huge list of ideas for improving the process. More importantly, the ideas will be the team's solutions and therefore more easily implemented.

Process Flow Diagram

Like the value stream map, the process flow diagram can be used to locate opportunity for improvement. In most cases, this

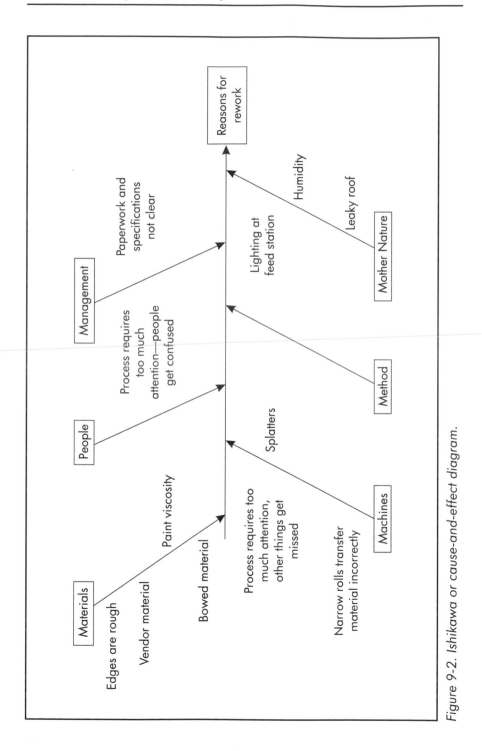

Figure 9-2. Ishikawa or cause-and-effect diagram.

Process	Warehouse	In-feed	Operator		
1. Quality specification					
2. Inspection frequency					
3. Inspection method					
4. Defect potential					
5. Potential cause					
6. Improvement ideas					
Results					

Figure 9-3. Sample of quality map.

tool is applied to identifying waste or causes for downtime, productivity, or stock-out issues. The tools for developing flowcharts can be as complex or simple as you decide. Software packages usually have templates and descriptions of what each symbol means. When work teams are developing problem-solving skills, simple is usually better.

Do not worry about format or whether the team is using the correct flow chart icon for showing a process, a document, or decision point. Allow the team have fun with it and let them use the tools to solve real problems rather than perfect the process of flow charting. Figure 9-4 shows a basic flow chart with a simple decision. In this example, my goal is to get to work on time. If early in the process I make a decision to press the snooze bar on my alarm clock radio, then I may skip the extra steps needed if the option to press the snooze bar was not exercised. When trying to visualize

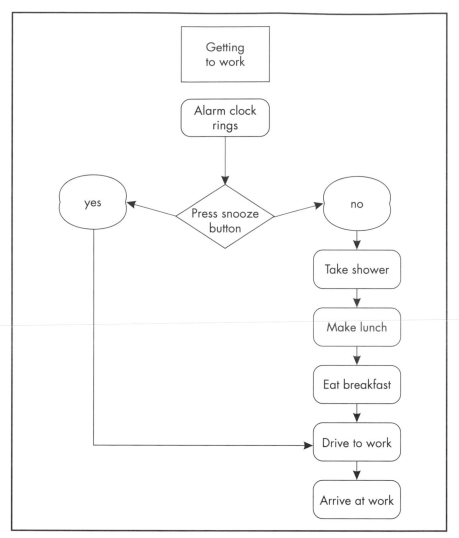

Figure 9-4. Process flow diagram.

process flows and decision points in a system, there are very few tools that work as well as process flow diagrams.

Did you notice that a critical step, getting dressed, was not documented on this flow chart? Overlooking such a critical step could be devastating. Identifying key operations and proper sequencing is one of the strengths of flow charting.

Deployment Flow Diagram

An alternative to the process flow diagram is the deployment flow diagram. The variation in this case is that when multiple operators or persons in the process have specific responsibilities at specific times, finding where a breakdown in communication or sequence is happening may need to be defined visually. Figure 9-5 demonstrates this by using the example of a customer going into a deli for coffee. If the customer does not go in or does not order coffee, the customer actions affect the entire process downstream.

Pareto Analysis

The Pareto graph is possibly the strongest tool in the toolbox for identifying what to work on first and for determining where to apply the tools. The Pareto graph is a very simple and visual tool for selecting and de-selecting projects in accordance with how meaningful they are to the team or the company.

Figure 9-6 shows a simple Pareto graph. The left-most bar shows that downtime caused by mechanical problems has the greatest potential for improvement. The next step might be to use the Ishikawa diagram to problem-solve the reason for downtime.

Studying another level of data on a Pareto chart may be necessary. For example, information that breaks down the reasons for mechanical downtime per day would look like that shown in Figure 9-7.

The ability to narrow down problems and the confidence that the right things are being addressed can have a powerful effect on team members. Without the visual data, these members might otherwise feel slighted or assume that the items they would like addressed are of greater importance.

Alternative Selection Worksheet

Once a team has brainstormed the problem and developed a few alternatives to choose from, you would think that the hard part is over. Actually, choosing between two or more worthy ideas can be very difficult and divisive for a team if not handled carefully. Having really creative people doesn't mean the choosing will

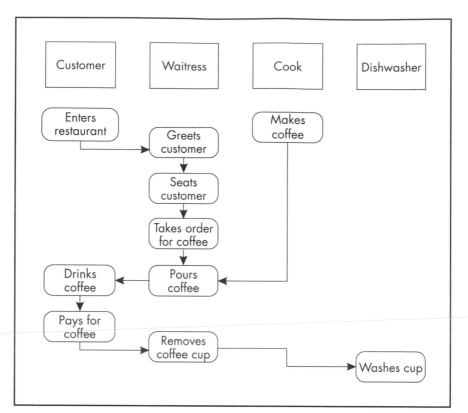

Figure 9-5. Deployment flow diagram.

be easier. Good brainstorming teams often come up with dozens of great ideas.

How can the team effectively narrow down the possibilities and select the best of the best? There is a tool that can help take some of the subjectivity, politics, and personality out of the decision-making process: consensus. If you use consensus, you will find that decision-making can happen rather quickly, and before you know it, the team will have a sound, objective decision that everyone can support. Using consensus rather than voting can be a very effective way to narrow the field without alienating anyone on the team. For consensus to work, everyone has to understand that they are not judging the value of the idea or the person who suggested it. The goal is to merely judge how effectively any one idea could be implemented at this moment in time.

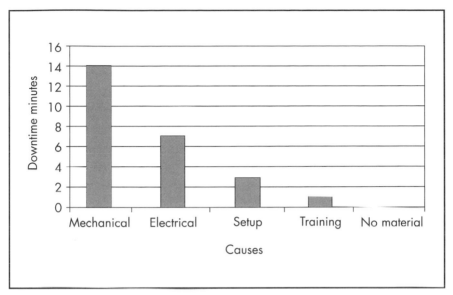

Figure 9-6. A simple Pareto chart.

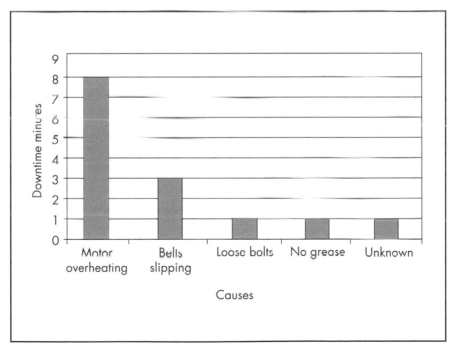

Figure 9-7. Pareto chart showing another level of data.

The criteria used to choose among many alternatives might vary with each project. For example, if the idea were related to a new machine purchase, cost would definitely be one of the criteria. In the case of a team working on alternatives for assigning standard work, cost may not have as great a role and might even be left off the list of selection criteria.

Table 9-1 shows three alternatives for a plant layout. The criteria used for this example might fit the example of Stan and his team choosing between three alternative cellular layouts.

In Table 9-1, one column is identified as "weighted value." This column is there in case one of the criteria is judged to be of greater importance than the rest. In this example, four of the criteria are judged to be equal. You could weight these criteria on a scale of 1-3, 1-5, or 1-10. Just make sure that they are all based on the same weighting scale.

The next step is to have the team rate each alternative for each criterion. The results of this are shown in Table 9-1 in the shaded columns. The number assigned as the weighted value is then multiplied against this number. The result of this multiplication is posted and then totaled. Having the team perform this as a group exercise gives all members a chance to express themselves and try to convince the group of any ideas they feel particularly strong about. The result after scoring is almost always the selection of the very best idea possible, with everyone buying into the solution and willing to give it a good try, since they participated in the process of selection.

There also might be an opportunity to create an additional alternative if two choices end up scoring identically. This new alternative might end up being the best solution if the team can glean the greatest good from the two highest scoring alternatives and generate a hybrid or compromise solution.

PROCESS CONTROL

You cannot have a discussion about quality without talking about process control. But that phrase sparks fear in the hearts of people who are not by nature statisticians or mathematicians. This section should humanize the techniques that have proven so positive to companies focusing on quality.

Table 9-1. Worksheet for alternative selection process

Selection Criteria	Weighted Value	Layout 1		Layout 2		Layout 3	
Impact on safety	3	3	9	2	6	3	9
Impact on quality	3	2	6	2	6	3	9
Cost	2	1	2	2	4	3	6
Allows flow	3	2	6	3	9	3	9
Allows line balancing	3	2	6	3	9	3	9
Time to implement	2	3	6	1	2	1	2
Total			35		36		44

The goal of business is to stay in business and profitability is part of that equation. The focus on quality, price, and delivery should drive us to make whatever improvements are necessary to fulfill customer needs while remaining profitable.

Some consultants are very good and have a broad understanding of how one discipline can support another. Others, trained or educated in a single discipline, tend to hold that practice as high as if it were a signal flag and deride any other approach or hybrid system of improvement. Having a particular science or technique well committed to memory is a fine thing, but understanding and being able to apply a wide variety of tools to help companies more consistently meet quality, price, and delivery objectives should be the goal.

There is always more than one solution to a problem. Solutions are found by appreciating the unique strengths of different disciplines, by capitalizing on the diversity of many different techniques and environments, and by applying a number of different approaches to different cultures and industries. The point is this: whatever the technique, program, or discipline, it must pass the test of logic, make the business better, and assist the organization in improving its goals of higher quality, lower cost (and therefore price), and improved delivery performance.

You can go overboard with any system, and you could have a system that has six-sigma capability. But if it doesn't help you stay in business, then what's the point? You could be the most capable company ever to go out of business. It comes down to balance. Be good at what you do and control your processes. Know your process capability and don't try to produce on a process that is incapable of meeting the needs of your customers. Know your limitations. Don't over-commit and under-deliver.

We can take the mystery out of process control for those who do not choose to sleep with calculators. The importance of process control can be inferred by a short analogy. Imagine that you own a three-year-old car. One day, someone backs into the fender of your car. When you take the car in for repair, the body shop informs you that they can't repair the damage and they will need to replace the fender. They will need to order another fender, and the new fender may have been manufactured weeks, months, or years after your car was built. If the process of making the new fender was "in control," the fender will fit. If there was variation in the process, if the process was "out of control," the fender will probably have gaps or the body shop personnel will have to deal with alignment problems.

Process control is the business of making sure that what you make will always be the same, whenever you make it, whoever makes it.

Customers begin to expect things a certain way. Even when things are better than they expect, if it is different for any reason, they will probably not be happy. For example, let's say that you go to a fast-food restaurant for a hamburger. An employee decides that homemade bread will make the sandwich taste better. As a customer expecting a certain product, you are dissatisfied. Even though the product might be much better, your expectation has not been met.

Process control would have us eliminate the variation so that the output is uniform and consistent. To develop a list of tools for making sure our processes are consistent and able to meet the customer's expectations, we should start by addressing all the potential causes of variation on the Ishikawa diagram (see Figure 9-2). For example, using the six potential causes of the Ishikawa process, we ask: what variation could be introduced by the information (management) system or how could the environment (Mother Nature) negatively affect the process? How could the method we use be modified to eliminate possible variation? Is it possible that the operators are capable of greater consistency in setup and process stability? What about the machines themselves? If all other conditions are equal, are the machines able to hold the tolerances required? Finally, could the materials used as input into the process be responsible for introducing a form of variation? The process of elimination, asking enough questions and acting on the answers, can eliminate reasons for variation one by one.

In most cases, the source of greatest variation is the human element. For example, at one time the precision sheet metal industry had this kind of variation built into the setup process. Because of smaller and smaller order quantities and lot sizes, the "hard" tooling that had been used for years in stamping equipment had became less profitable. "Soft" tooling used in new computer numerically controlled press brakes had come to provide greater flexibility.

Soft tooling is tooling that costs hundreds of dollars and can be cut into many small pieces, enabling the operator to set it up in many different configurations. Hard tooling (such as that used in huge stamping presses) still has its place, but can cost thousands of dollars and does not provide a great deal of flexibility for small lot sizes or short life-cycle products.

The variation in the process was that each operator was able to take this soft tooling and develop his/her own "capable" setup. The ownership of these operator-specific setups was strong. Being expert setup people, they took a lot of pride in their setup design. It was a form of engineering, and when they found a process that worked, they stayed with it. Some operators even went out of their way to keep other operators from learning their solution to particularly difficult setups, thus satisfying a personal perception that "what only I know makes me more valuable."

The first few recommendations to begin the process of standardizing setups or developing "best practices" fell on deaf ears. Operators were hiding setup books in their toolboxes or sometimes even moving to other companies rather than sharing their knowledge. They were so used to the old practice of reinventing individualized setups each time that many were unable to make the transition.

Strictly from an economic standpoint, the application of best practices or standard operating procedures began to demonstrate the benefits of controlling the process. It was only logical that it would have to be less expensive to provide an operator with a prepared document that recommended a particular set of tools rather than reinventing the wheel each time the setup was performed.

From a quality perspective, the consistency would also have to be better. Looking at it from the customer's viewpoint, the delivery performance would improve if the setups were happening faster and more reliably. Cost, quality, delivery—it all gets better, and before long, there is no way the customer can afford to go elsewhere.

Setup sheets have now become a way of life in the precision sheet metal industry. Yet there are still shops that do not use them. Some operators argue that best practices stifle creativity.

The Lean way of thinking would be to encourage creativity by inviting operators to challenge a setup if they feel that they have a better way to do it. Once proven, change the best practice. Why should we risk customer satisfaction because only one operator has the knowledge or is the only one who can perform the setup? The goal must be that it works for everyone. Otherwise, sooner or later, the customer will be dissatisfied because of product variation.

Figure 9-8 shows an example of a setup sheet for a press brake (bending or forming) machine.

Another form of documenting best practice is to develop a written procedure or work instruction. Many companies today are seeking to become registered as compliant to ISO 9000, the quality standard from the International Organization for Standardization (ISO). The automotive version is QS 9000. ISO is an international body that works on standardizing issues to develop a common understanding about topics critical to all countries. ISO 9000 is a system that was developed in Europe and has grown in popularity in the United States over the last 20 years. ISO 9000 provides a means for everyone to operate on the same playing field.

Procedures and work instructions can serve multiple purposes, such as defining the process and measuring whether people know it and are fulfilling the requirements as defined.

ISO developed 20 items to guide companies through the process of standardizing their quality systems. Once a company has addressed all 20 items and has performed its own audit of the system, it can request an independent audit by a certified ISO auditor. If approved, the company can be recommended for certification.

ISO certification judges the processes within the company to be capable and in control of quality. Most registrars (certification companies) perform a set of scheduled and mutually agreed-upon surveillance audits to ensure continued compliance. Every three years or so, the entire certification process is repeated.

Within the ISO structure, three primary levels of documents guide each employee toward a thorough understanding of the steps necessary to control their processes. To some people this seems restrictive. However, ISO does not say what to do. Each company and each work unit merely needs to define its own process. Within reason, the system is as restrictive or as flexible as desired. Just as in preschool, some kids are just too creative to stay in the lines when they color. Some companies are so dynamic that using an

Press Brake Setup Sheet

Sketch part here if required to show special bend sequence, etc.	Book #:
	Page #:
	Tape #:
	Side ___ Block ___ Step ___
	Customer print #:
	Developed by:
	Approved by:
	Date:

Sketch tooling setup> > > > >

# Flange	Depth	Option	Option
1			
2			
3			
4			
5			
6			
7			
8			
9			
10			
11			
12			
13			
14			

Customer name:	
	Punch type:
	❑ Std ❑ Acute ❑ Gsnk
Part #:	Reversed ❑ Yes ❑ No
Part name:	Special (describe):
Current revision level:	Special tool location:
Inside tooling:	
❑Y ❑N	Die opening:
❑ Bolster	❑ Single 'V' ❑ Double 'V'
❑ Punch	'V' toward: ❑ Front ❑ Rear
❑ Die	1 in. extensions back stop #
Packaging notes:	❑ 1 ❑ 2 ❑ 3 ❑ 4
	Die protection:
	❑ Yes ❑ No

Part history:

Operator	Quantity	Date	Comments

Doc #	F9.04	Rev	03/02/00	Page 1 of 1	Approval:

Forming notes: _____

Figure 9-8. Example of a press brake setup sheet.

ISO 9000 program from another company would feel like wearing a straightjacket. If the lines of your quality system are too restrictive, move the line. It is not ISO's line. It is yours.

Figures 9-9 and 9-10 are forms for sample procedures with work instructions. Procedures generally apply to more than one department. Work instructions support the procedures and are usually machine, department, or work-cell specific.

Pre-control

Another tool for ensuring the ongoing quality of material produced is the pre-control method.

If the goal is to find a tool that people will use, make it easy to understand. Conversely, make the process difficult, and you almost guarantee that people will misuse the documents, because they do not understand or see the value in using them as tools to help them.

A sample of a pre-control chart is shown in Figure 9-11. The strength of this chart is its simplicity. Table 9-2 is an example of a military specification (mil spec.) sampling plan commonly used in job shop environments. Note that sampling plans can differ based on customer tolerances, acceptable quality limits, and inspection frequency requirements.

Figure 9-11 shows a simple pre-control chart commonly used by machine operators to assist them in determining when to make an adjustment to their machine and when to leave it alone. The target is the dimension required by the blueprint or specification. Zone 1 is a plus or minus value that is assigned in any increment. The operator plots the resulting measurement from the first unit in the first column, repeating the process for the first five units produced, moving one column to the right for each unit measured. If each of the first five units falls between the upper Zone 1 and the lower Zone 1, then he/she can begin measuring every fifth unit. When the 30th unit has been produced, and if none of the units have fallen outside Zone 1, then the operator can measure every 25th unit until the end of the run.

If at any time a unit falls within Zone 2, the next five units must be measured. If a second unit within this group of five falls within Zone 2, an adjustment is made and the process of measuring

In-process Inspection		
Procedure Responsibility	Step	Action
		Normal production
Production personnel	1.0	Receive work order and product to work on.
	1.1	Review work order and product to ensure: • previous operations and required tests have been performed and signed off; • required quantity is correct; • work order number and product match; and • shelf-life sensitive materials are not expired. (If one or more of these conditions are false, contact supervisor prior to production.)
	1.2	Review work order and/or setup instructions for test or inspections required for his/her work center.
	1.3	At process completion, sign and date work order and identify: • the test status of the project; • operator and date of completion; • location where parts are stored (if applicable); and • quantity of parts successfully processed.
Production personnel	1.4	Prototype production
		The first "good" part is either taken to Quality Assurance Department for first article inspection or the inspection is performed by authorized personnel if directed to do so in writing on the work order by sales or production manager.
Inspection personnel	1.5	If nonconformances are found, see ACME document number.
	1.6	Sign and date work order and identify the same information listed in 1.3. Note: engineering prototypes used to qualify designs may not be accompanied by a work order.
ACME Doc # WI0.02 Rev 03/02/00 Page 1 of 1 Approval:		

Figure 9-9. Sample of an in-process inspection sheet.

Turret Punch Operation		
Responsibility	Step	Activity
Programmer	1.0	Determine machine schedule based on due dates.
	1.1	Send numerical control (NC) program to machine via modem or disk, assign unique number to program (record number on setup sheet).
Lead person	1.2	Assign job to operator.
	1.3	Provide operator the following (but not limited to) information: • Blueprint; and • Router (job traveler).
Operator	1.4	Log onto job in "Fabritrak" system.
	1.5	Follow instructions on setup sheet and router.
	1.6	Review blueprint, work order, and setup sheet (ensure that all revision levels match). For repeat jobs, find flat pattern template.
	1.7	Select and install tooling.
	1.8	Call up NC program from machine or disk memory.
	1.9	Test run part.
	2.0	Visually inspect part for cosmetic quality and check part dimensionally (on both sides) against pattern. Check the results of each forming tool (for example, countersinks, letter stamps, etc.).
	2.1	Make necessary adjustments, including sharpening tools when deemed necessary (go to 1.9 if adjustments are made).
	2.2	Obtain part approval from authorized inspection personnel (generally lead person or shop supervisor).
Inspection personnel	2.3	Perform first article inspection.
	2.4	Where appropriate, identify critical features to monitor in addition to those specified on the work order.
	2.5	Sign work order, signifying approval or make recommendation to operator to go back to step 2.1.
Operator	2.6	Run job.
	2.7	Perform 100% cosmetic inspection on both sides of each sheet after processing. Dimensionally check parts against pattern (see ACME sampling plan to determine number of parts to inspect).
	2.8	Record statistical data (see "pre-control" chart) related to critical dimensions if instructions to do so appear on the work order.
	2.9	Interweave parts with paper or separate with cardboard if instructed to do so on the work order.
	3.0	Stack parts all one way (if possible) to reduce chances of misinterpreting orientation on downstream operations.
	3.1	If a part is identified as reject, write "TEST", or "SETUP" with permanent marker (or tag), or throw part in scrap container. (Note: next operation may need setup pieces.)
	3.2	Log off job on "Fabritrak" system.
	3.3	When completing job, record acceptable quantity complete.
	3.4	Attach print or tag to parts identifying them and notify the lead person or shop supervisor of job completion.
ACME Doc # WI9.04 Rev 02/04/00 Page 1 of 1 Approval:		

Figure 9-10. Sample of procedure instructions sheet.

Customer	Customer #	Work order #

Part name	Print #	Operator

	1-5	6-25	26-100

Zone 3
0	0	0	0	0	0	0	0	0	0	0	0	0	0	0
0	0	0	0	0	0	0	0	0	0	0	0	0	0	0
0	0	0	0	0	0	0	0	0	0	0	0	0	0	0
0	0	0	0	0	0	0	0	0	0	0	0	0	0	0
0	0	0	0	0	0	0	0	0	0	0	0	0	0	0

Zone 2
0	0	0	0	0	0	0	0	0	0	0	0	0	0	0
0	0	0	0	0	0	0	0	0	0	0	0	0	0	0
0	0	0	0	0	0	0	0	0	0	0	0	0	0	0
0	0	0	0	0	0	0	0	0	0	0	0	0	0	0
0	0	0	0	0	0	0	0	0	0	0	0	0	0	0

Zone 1
0	0	0	0	0	0	0	0	0	0	0	0	0	0	0
0	0	0	0	0	0	0	0	0	0	0	0	0	0	0
0	0	0	0	0	0	0	0	0	0	0	0	0	0	0
0	0	0	0	0	0	0	0	0	0	0	0	0	0	0
0	0	0	0	0	0	0	0	0	0	0	0	0	0	0

Target
| 0 | 0 | 0 | 0 | 0 | 0 | 0 | 0 | 0 | 0 | 0 | 0 | 0 | 0 | 0 |

Zone 1
0	0	0	0	0	0	0	0	0	0	0	0	0	0	0
0	0	0	0	0	0	0	0	0	0	0	0	0	0	0
0	0	0	0	0	0	0	0	0	0	0	0	0	0	0
0	0	0	0	0	0	0	0	0	0	0	0	0	0	0
0	0	0	0	0	0	0	0	0	0	0	0	0	0	0

Zone 2
0	0	0	0	0	0	0	0	0	0	0	0	0	0	0
0	0	0	0	0	0	0	0	0	0	0	0	0	0	0
0	0	0	0	0	0	0	0	0	0	0	0	0	0	0
0	0	0	0	0	0	0	0	0	0	0	0	0	0	0
0	0	0	0	0	0	0	0	0	0	0	0	0	0	0

Zone 3
0	0	0	0	0	0	0	0	0	0	0	0	0	0	0
0	0	0	0	0	0	0	0	0	0	0	0	0	0	0
0	0	0	0	0	0	0	0	0	0	0	0	0	0	0
0	0	0	0	0	0	0	0	0	0	0	0	0	0	0
0	0	0	0	0	0	0	0	0	0	0	0	0	0	0

Figure 9-11. Sample pre-control chart.

the first five parts starts over again. This continues until the process is stable again and all parts are falling within Zone 1.

If at any time a part is found to be within Zone 3, all parts produced since the last inspection are re-inspected. If a second unit is found outside Zone 1, an investigation as to why the process is vary-

Table 9-2. Military specification sampling plan

Lot size quantity	Sample Size
1–3	3
4–25	5
26–50	6
51–150	7
150–280	10
281–500	11
501–1,200	15
1,201–3,200	18
3,201–10,000	22
10,001–150,000	29

ing is undertaken. Adjustments are made and the process of measuring the first five parts is repeated to ensure that all parts fall within Zone 1.

If the measured units fall randomly on either side of the target and outside Zone 1, the operator probably needs to change the setup until the process proves capable. Table 9-2 shows a sampling plan.

C_P/C_{PK}

There is a measurement that many companies are focusing on as an indicator of process capability. This measurement is known as C_P (process capability) or C_{PK} (process capability index). Roughly translated, C_{PK} is an indicator of process capability. Another definition is that C_{PK} is an estimate of the statistical probability that a process will be capable of producing parts within an acceptable limit of defects in the future, based on process performance of the past.

In Tables 9-3 and 9-4, there are 25 measurements representing what is generally regarded to be a statistically sound sample size. These measurements are used to calculate the statistical results appearing on the right side of the tables.

The C_{PK} index in Table 9-4 is 1.069. The C_{PK} index in Table 9-3 is 2.671. The higher the C_{PK} number, the more capable the process

Table 9-3. Process capability worksheet

Part #	123		Customer name	XYZ
Rev #	B		Target	1.000
WO #	321		Upper specification	1.010
Tolerance	0.010		Lower specification	0.990

Measurements

1	0.999		X-bar	0.998
2	0.999		Range	0.002
3	0.997		Standard deviation	0.001
4	0.999		Specified tolerance	0.020
5	0.999		C_p index	3.290
6	0.999		UCL	1.003
7	0.999		LCL	0.997
8	0.999		Z_{max}	11.72
9	0.999		Z_{min}	8.01
10	0.999		C_{pk} index	2.671
11	0.999		C_p index	3.290
12	0.997			
13	0.997			
14	0.997			
15	0.997			
16	0.997			
17	0.997			
18	0.997			
19	0.997			
20	0.997			
21	0.999			
22	0.999			
23	0.999			
24	0.999			
25	0.997			

has shown itself. The reason for this difference is that the dimensions recorded in the measurement column of Table 9-3 are slightly more consistent than in Table 9-4.

The threshold for judging a process as capable is around 1.3. Any process lower than 1.3 is assumed to be incapable of reliably making a product to the specification.

So, what does C_{PK} really mean to the customer when they ask for a C_{PK} index for a particular machine or process? Statistical Process Control (SPC) and hammers are just tools. I do not care

Table 9-4. Another process capability worksheet

Part #	123		Customer name	XYZ
Rev #	B		Target	1.000
WO #	321		Upper specification	1.010
Tolerance	0.010		Lower specification	0.990

Measurements

1	0.995	X-bar	0.997	
2	0.999	Range	0.007	
3	0.995	Standard deviation	0.002	
4	0.999	Specified tolerance	0.020	
5	0.995	C_p index	1.571	
6	0.999	UCL	1.006	
7	0.999	LCL	0.994	
8	0.999	Z_{max}	6.22	
9	0.999	Z_{min}	3.21	
10	0.999	C_{pk} index	1.069	
11	0.994	C_p index	1.571	
12	0.997			
13	0.997			
14	0.994			
15	0.997			
16	0.997			
17	0.992			
18	0.997			
19	0.997			
20	0.997			
21	0.999			
22	0.994			
23	0.994			
24	0.999			
25	0.997			

how a hammer is made; I just want to pound in a nail. Give me enough information to be able to interpret the data or safely swing the hammer and then get out of my way. I think most operators would agree.

Think of C_{PK} as a weather barometer: the higher the air pressure, the better the weather (generally). The way you measure pressure in a barometer is to watch the fluid rise in a tube. Basically, the C_{PK} barometer works the same way. Watching the statistical data rise inside or fall outside a certain range can tell you a lot about the process.

Table 9-5 shows a histogram of a manufacturing process. Each part measured is plotted on the chart and begins to form a distribution. The distribution shape can tell you a lot about the process. However, while it can give you an indication, it cannot tell you the true process capability based on customer expectations or specifications.

The range that ultimately defines process capability is the tolerance. As the tolerance becomes tighter and tighter, the need for capability increases, and any variation or deviation from the target shows up as a lower C_{PK} index.

Statisticians will be familiar with the term *sigma*, the mathematical and statistical term for "standard deviation." Here is an

Table 9-5. Histogram of a manufacturing process

Frequency	0.992	0.993	0.994	0.995	0.996	0.997	0.998	0.999	1.000	1.001	1.002	1.003	1.004	1.005	1.006	1.007	1.008
17																	
16																	
15																	
14																	
13																	
12								X									
11								X									
10								X									
9								X									
8								X									
7								X									
6								X	X								
5								X	X	X							
4							X	X	X	X							
3							X	X	X	X	X						
2						X	X	X	X	X	X						
1						X	X	X	X	X	X	X					

example of a formula for calculating the standard deviation of a set of data:

$$\Sigma\,(X - \bar{X})^2 \qquad\qquad (9\text{-}1)$$

$$S^2 = n - 1$$

where:

Σ = sum total
n = total number of items
X = each item
S^2 = mean squared deviation

The first step in calculating a C_{PK} index is to know the sigma limits. There are many mathematical processes for calculating a sigma limit. Think about a sigma limit as the zones we looked at in Figure 9-11. Using this same pre-control sheet, we will apply four zones instead of three and substitute the term sigma for zone. If we divide the customer specifications into eight equal zones, four on each side of the target, a tolerance of 0.020 in. (.5 mm) would be divided into eight zones. Each zone would be 0.005 in. (.127 mm). By placing these zones on each side of the target, as shown in Figure 9-12, we can use them to help identify an ap proximate C_{PK} index for the process.

If all the parts we measure are normally (equally and uniformly) distributed around the target and fall within three of the four zones, then the process has a statistical likelihood of producing good parts somewhere around 99.73 percent of the time. This translates to a C_{PK} of about 1.3.

The key is that all the parts must first fall within a normal distribution. It serves no purpose to calculate a C_{PK} for a process that you know is out of control.

The operators can use the zones (or sigma limits) to visually approximate the C_{PK} index. A distribution of measurements that is centered on the target and stays within Zone 3 will be somewhere between 1 and 2 C_{PK}. A distribution that is centered on and remains within the limits of Zone 2 will have a C_{PK} of around 2 or higher. If all measurements are centered on the target and stay within Zone 1, then the C_{PK} index will be somewhere around three. The higher the number, the greater the reliability. It's not rocket

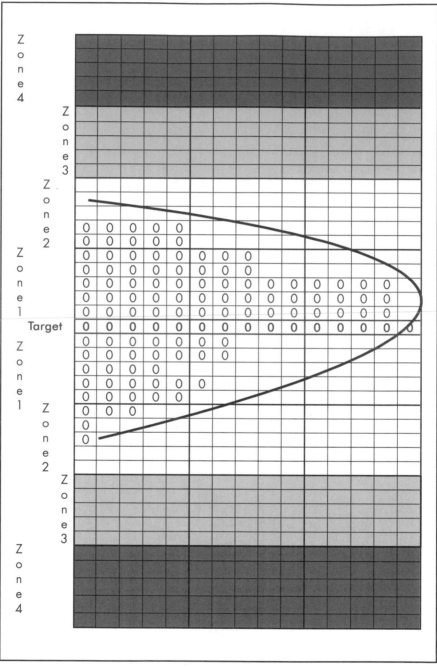

Figure 9-12. Zones are assigned to get the approximate C_{PK} index.

science, even though some people will try to overcomplicate it. A C_{PK} of 1.3 is considered very good. Having a C_{PK} higher than 1.3 indicates that you have a very capable process and you might be able to tighten up your tolerances. Figures 9-13, 9-14, and 9-15 are graphic representations of what C_P and C_{PK} try to identify.

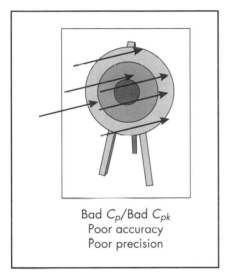

Bad C_p/Bad C_{pk}
Poor accuracy
Poor precision

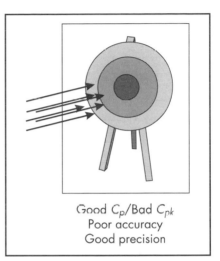

Good C_p/Bad C_{pk}
Poor accuracy
Good precision

Figure 9-13. Poor accuracy and poor precision result in bad C_P and C_{PK}.

Figure 9-14. Poor accuracy and good precision result in good C_P but bad C_{PK}.

BUDDY CHECK

Having each operator responsible for checking the previous work center's output quality is a simple system for verifying that proper attention to the quality system has been provided each production run. Of course, this process works only in real time; it's too late if a process produces all the components in a batch before the buddy check happens.

SUMMARY

Beauty and quality are in the eye of the beholder. The customers (internal and external) are the ones who should set the

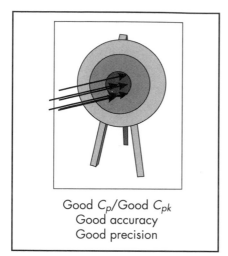

Good C_p/Good C_{pk}
Good accuracy
Good precision

Figure 9-15. With good accuracy and precision, you should get both good C_P and C_{PK}.

expectations. If we give customers more than they need and charge them for it because we are overcontrolling the process, our customers will not be happy if they find out about it. On the other hand, if we give them less than they expect, even if we sell it to them for less, they will again be unhappy. We must focus on customer needs, specifications, and expectations in regard to product condition, price, delivery, and quality. If we do these things, how can we go wrong?

Training teams to use statistical tools is a fine thing. That's why we hire quality assurance managers to train and implement these tools.

Bring the folks in the shop along at a rate they can absorb. Give them the hammer or the SPC tool and show them how to safely use it. They do not need to become genetic engineers to demonstrate that they are in control of their process.

10

People Make a Difference

It has always been my position that if you do not genuinely care about people, hire someone who does. You must have genuine concern, heartfelt respect, and commitment to every single employee in your plant. You must give the simple and sincere honor due to each person, not just as a work associate, but as a fellow human being. Unless these fundamental needs are met, no amount of Lean technologies will make a significant and sustainable difference in your company's performance.

People in the organization should be treated as if there were no one else on earth with their unique combination of skills, ideas, and personality. If, whenever they have an idea, they are given a chance to fully express themselves . . . if they are offered feedback, both positive and corrective, always with regard to maintaining their self-esteem . . . if they are acknowledged for their efforts . . . if they are recognized as being a critical part of the team . . . if they are offered the opportunity to learn and grow personally . . . if they feel so connected to their team that when they drive by the plant, they are sure in their hearts that they are directly responsible for the continuing success of the company . . . then and only then, will they be in a mental state to offer and risk everything they have to be a team player.

If you bypass the emotional needs of people to get all you can out of them at one time, with little or no regard to the effect on their emotional bank accounts, the result is a very expensive and shortsighted way to do business.

UNDOING NEGATIVE ACTIONS

There is an algebraic expression that well summarizes interactions with people: $1n = 17p$. To translate, every negative action takes 17 positive actions to undo.

Child psychologists conducting emotional tests with very young children found that yelling at them had long-lasting negative effects. For example, if in a moment of haste or rage I shout at my child, "Johnny, you little brat, you make me so mad! Why can't you be more like Jimmy?" The study demonstrated that the damage to the delicate relationship between parent and child cannot be undone by one, two, or three equally endearing and heartfelt expressions of validation. Undoing or restoring emotional equilibrium is not done on a one-to-one ratio. It will take an average of 17 positive reinforcements just to bring the relationship back to the level experienced previous to the negative outburst.

As a parent, I must examine the long-term cost of bypassing the process of communication. It is the most important thing I can do. If I ignore this principle, if I do not give this formula the attention it deserves, it may happen that some time in the future, quietly, silently, maybe indiscernibly, the relationship with my child is damaged beyond complete repair.

The reality of the human spirit does not change just because we get older. If someone hurts us deeply, it doesn't matter whether we are 4 or 44 years old. When the hurt happens, the $1n = 17p$ formula surfaces and is as strong and inescapable as gravity. Regardless of our station in life, when someone abuses our emotional needs, the relationship is damaged at some level.

As managers, team members, and peers, we need to ask ourselves whether the firefight that we find ourselves in at work every day is reason enough to shortcut the process with people. Should we risk the relationships that may have taken years or a lifetime to build? If we want teams that care about each other and if we want the success of the company, we must set the example. We must show respect, consistency, frankness, truthfulness, and a high regard for the self-esteem of everyone at every level of the organization.

HELPING PEOPLE DO GREAT WORK

The goal is to bring out the best in people, and to do so requires a good understanding of them. We will now discuss how choice can be used as a tool to create business people; how to develop the entrepreneurial spirit; what makes a businessperson; and wage structures.

Choice: A Tool to Create Business People

Most business managers, owners, and even department leaders fail to perform the very necessary exercise of putting themselves in the place of those they lead. If a leader has not personally walked in the shoes of those he leads, or if it has been a long time since he was an hourly employee, it is extremely easy to take their position for granted. It is easy to forget what it feels like to have limited choices.

One reason companies and managers hesitate to enfranchise employees is that bad decisions can be expensive. Great decision-makers are not just born. It is a learned behavior. If managers will take an honest look back in time, they will have to admit that they made some bad decisions on their way to becoming good decision-makers.

It takes time and experience to develop work teams and it takes time and practice for work teams to mature into business units capable of assuming decision-making responsibilities. A team development continuum will be discussed in Chapter 12.

Freedom and power of choice are the greatest privileges and best feelings in the world. People fight and die for freedom every day in all parts of the world. Yet, it is probable that 80 percent of the people in the working world do not have a true sense of choice in their everyday job. Some people do have choices in life and they may abuse them or make wrong choices. In any case, it is not right to label or punish the majority for the mistakes of a minority.

The Entrepreneurial Spirit

Just as it is unfair for a parent to expect a child to act like a grown-up, it is unreasonable for business owners and managers to expect hourly employees to act as business-minded individuals.

It has been said that the 80-20 percent rule applies to many things in nature, but also applies to people, finances, and a host of other activities in life. With regard to people's motivations, not everyone born into a family business demonstrates the necessary spirit and energy required to keep the family vision alive. And equally true is the statement that not everyone working in the trenches is satisfied with their situation.

If given the vision, resources, incentives, skills through proper training, and the opportunity, a greater percentage of people will rise to meet the challenge required to become fully enfranchised and contributing members of an organization.

Just as with a child, with teams there is a formative period. Developing teams into effective business units requires patience and coaching. How people are treated at work and how their self-esteem is maintained (or not) will largely determine how much and how effectively they choose to participate. We can never know a person's full potential until he/she is given a chance to fully perform. Managers may not realize that many people, thinking it rude to demand that chance, stay in the trench, keep their heads down, and remain undiscovered diamonds. We have an opportunity to create a diamond mine.

What Makes a Businessperson?

What does a businessperson bring to a business? Does he/she bring an MBA degree, practical experience, financial backing, intuitive decision-making abilities, endless stockpiles of energy, vision, a marketing plan, perspiration, and concern for the customer? Of course, it would be ideal if the person had the entire package. It is no wonder that so many new businesses fail in the first few years. Regardless of good intentions, it takes a very special person to succeed in business. It takes someone who is a risk-taker, someone who has the determination to plan, begin, stay with it, and succeed.

How can employees ever hope to feel the desire and satisfaction that business owners feel? How can they ever hope to develop something they feel that they can call their own? How can we hope to instill within them the same entrepreneurial spirit or create an environment where they experience the same feelings of satisfaction that an owner feels? How can we coach them to become owner-operators of their own business, making owner-like decisions, and taking owner-like actions as if they were running it for themselves? Simple: we must offer them a choice.

The only things most employees have to offer are their skills, ability to think, and willingness to apply effort to a job. They don't have vast resources of money (otherwise they might start their own business). They generally lack the higher education that might provide them a more lucrative position in business.

While good decision making can be a learned behavior, they often cannot claim these skills because they have never had the chance to develop them. All they have to offer is themselves; this is their entire package. Their willingness to trade time for money is their personal stake in the business. How can we use this principle to generate more excitement within our employed associates?

The difference between someone perceived to be a team player (a business-minded individual) and someone who just keeps his/her head down in the trench is often determined within the first few work experiences. The new employee may offer suggestions or try to demonstrate an idea for improvement. How those first few efforts are received can create a pattern for the rest of his/her working life. The cost of a manager not responding appropriately can be immeasurable.

Most companies do a good job managing the materials. Raw material costs are usually the greatest percentage of the cost pie and thus receive a good deal of attention. Buildings, tools, and machinery are generally so important to an operation that they get the mindful attention they deserve. Variable spending is also usually well managed. But, the human resource is not always measured or managed on the same plane.

Some organizations demonstrate a genuine respect for their employees. However, shortsighted leaders, managers, and owners sometimes view people as little more than an easily replaced commodity. When managers are honest with themselves, they recognize that regardless of the technologies and materials available, without the best efforts of people, the results will be marginal.

Sure, there will always be people willing to give an honest day's work for a wage. But, to generate the sustained level of performance and enthusiasm that superstars or championship teams exude takes a special kind of relationship. It takes recognition and, above all, mutual respect between employer and employee.

One of the most powerful ways to demonstrate and build respect is to create an environment where people have choice. This choice must provide a sense of control over not only their day-to-day duties but their destiny. This includes an influence over their compensation package.

When employees are compensated on the basis of how well they perform against very specific goals and a clearly defined set of measurements, they become keenly aware of their performance and the performance of their peers. They begin seeking, in fact demanding the removal of non-value-added and redundant tasks or worthless paperwork that slows them down. Instead of gravitating toward the easiest jobs, a program of this type encourages people to grow in knowledge and skill to seek the most demanding roles.

The measurement and perception of what represents the best position in the plant will change from how easy the job is to how closely a position utilizes and tests a person's total package of skills and abilities. This is a major shift from current systems that encourage employees to "work up to" the easiest role, finding the ideal position that provides a resting place until retirement.

Hourly employees have only their selves, their skills, and their abilities acquired over a lifetime to offer as a business resource. If treated like a commodity and expected to give 110 percent simply for the satisfaction of trading time for dollars, people will generally perform to the lower level of expectation. All they have to offer is themselves, and there is probably a tendency to reserve something for later.

To expect employees to give their all in an environment that does not appreciate or reward effort would be like a customer expecting a business to give products away or sell products at a ridiculously low margin. Your company would probably not put its heart and soul into satisfying that kind of customer. If appreciated and rewarded appropriately, employees will feel respected and begin operating in a manner that makes themselves and the company as profitable as possible.

Wage Structures for the New Century

A fundamental need in any company is a compensation package that offers people a greater sense of choice and recognizes effort while rewarding high performance. Traditional job descriptions are a holdover from the past. To paint lines around people by saying, "You are a press brake operator" or "You are a vertical mill operator" is to limit their potential. This section will present an alternative.

Note: For those who work in companies with third-party employee representation, please reserve judgement until the end of this chapter. This process works in unionized environments as well as in non-union shops.

For the sake of simplicity, let's assume that there are dozens of current job descriptions in The Jobbe Shoppe, owned by Stan and Fran. Table 10-1 shows how they might identify people in the plant by job title and wage. Traditional departmental or functional operating disciplines would no doubt have Mel T. Steel welding large batches of material at a time. If he runs out of something to weld, he might have to go home or move to another weld station where there is something else to weld. Because his job title is welder and he is highly skilled in that one function, most companies would try to capitalize on his skill 100 percent of the time.

When Stan and his team reconfigure into a cellular layout, the need to weld full time may become less important, and Mel's flexibility will become more important. Sometimes there is hesitancy on the part of both management and the operator, who have for so long both been focused on a perceived need for the operator to stay busy in his/her area of expertise.

Table 10-1. Traditional job description and wage chart

Department	Job Title	Employee	Wage
Fab	Press brake operator	I.L. Bendum	$10.15
Weld	Welder	Mel T. Steel	$12.50
Hardware	Hardware installer	Preston Nutt	$ 8.25
Punch	Turret punch operator	Imaak Houles	$ 9.75

Fear or lack of motivation to learn new things is another reason for foot dragging when it comes to cross training. Here are some tools to help motivate people to share and seek knowledge.

By changing the compensation system to reward rather than restrict mobility and cross-functionality, we can fully expect to see a self-perpetuating system develop that impels people to outperform the old titled job system and departmental sub-optimization.

I am going to discuss a method that takes the subjectivity out of the process of determining wage rates, while allowing people to have a greater measure of control over their destiny and compensation package. It has the effect of making each person in the plant responsible for running "their business" as profitably as possible. In the process, the entire business is then made more profitable.

Break each job down into three categories: the physical nature, the mental nature or demand, and the technical aspect. We should then be able to define the relative value of each job to the organization. The more value-added the job is, the more financially rewarding. To attract the greatest skill sets to the areas most demanding these abilities, the company must recognize the need to compensate according to the level of value-added and effort required.

Table 10-2 uses the same names as in Table 10-1 but has an additional four columns in which the physical, mental, technical, and leadership demands of each job or set of tasks is rated. Notice that there is no longer a column identifying a department and there are no job titles. Instead, there are typical job duties as defined in the standard work. There are also no wage assignments, but an area is included to calculate the overall value of the job to the team.

How can each of the categories be objectively and fairly judged? Table 10-3 provides an example of how each category can be broken down into measurable criteria. Some companies may choose to add criteria related to output expectations, thus providing goals that are measurable. Whatever system you develop, it should be one that allows people to easily understand what the expectation is, and provides them with a sense of control and choice.

Dividing the wage structure into manageable steps, levels, or degrees will allow people to set attainable goals and experience the satisfaction of moving through a career rather than just showing up every day for a job.

Table 10-2. Revised job description chart

Standard work	Employee	Physical	Mental	Technical	Leadership	Total
Scale　　　　　>>>		0–6	0–6	0–6	0–6	
Relative importance >>>	Multiplier	1	2	3	4	
Operate press brake Perform setups Perform quality checks Assist team in managing standard work-in-process (WIP) Provide cross-training for brake operation 5-S (sort, straighten, shine, standardize, sustain) and preventive maintenance	I.L. Bendum	3	4	2	2	25
Weld Assist hardware installation Perform external setup activities Perform quality checks	Mel T. Steel					
Install hardware Package Maintain finished goods inventory (FGI)	Preston Nutt					
Turret punch operator Move material from shear area to cell Maintain team visuals	Imaak Houles					

Table 10-4 shows a spreadsheet with sample wages and all the calculations for scoring a job.

A *cross-training matrix* can be implemented as a visual tool to identify each team member's level of skill. This tool allows the team to plan who will learn what and the order needed to ensure

Table 10-3. Job description chart showing demand criteria

Physical Requirement	Mental Requirement	Technical Requirement
Pace	Retention	Interprets specifications, blueprints, and BOMs
Bending/twisting	Repetition	
Repetition	Attention to detail	Complex measurements
Weight	Avoid snow-blindness	Machine adjustments
Environment	Need to think ahead	Setup sheets
Endurance	Communication	Troubleshooting
Demand to set the pace	Paperwork accuracy	Flexibility/multi-tasking
	Quality awareness	Visualize new products/ processes
	Safety awareness	SPC charting
		Machine maintenance
		Need to train others

that the training happens. The goal is to have each person fully qualified on at least two pieces of equipment, and to have at least two people to operate each piece of equipment. Figure 10-1 shows the cross-training matrix.

Is There a Downside?

Some potentially negative scenarios can arise during the implementation of a program such as the one just described. The reason for pointing this out is that no program should be implemented in a vacuum. To measure productivity alone, without consideration for safety, quality, or morale can be counterproductive.

Once people begin to feel that they are truly in charge of their destiny, some may tend to go overboard, such as taking on too much responsibility, taking shortcuts on safety, or possibly causing injury to themselves by working too hard. Burnout is also a real possibility in the second and third year if they attempt to take on too much. Rotation and cross training can become a preventive tool at this point.

Another concern could be that focusing only on productivity might increase the number of neglected maintenance items. There

Table 10-4. Worksheet showing job demand and wages

Department	Job Description	Physical Demand	Mental Demand	Technical Demand	Leadership Demand	Points	Rating	Current	Revised
Punch	Operator	3	3	4	2	29	8	$10.00	$10.50
Weld	Operator	2	4	3	2	27	8	$11.00	$10.50
Hardware	Apprentice	2	3	3	0	17	8	$9.00	$8.50
Form	Operator	4	4	4	2	32	8	$12.00	$10.50
Punch	Lead person	2	4	5	3	37	8	$13.00	$11.75
Form	Lead person	3	5	6	4	47	8	$13.00	$12.25
Form	Apprentice	2	2	2	0	12	8	$8.00	$7.75
Hardware	Department lead	2	5	4	6	48	8	$12.00	$12.75
Paint	Painter	4	3	3	2	27	8	$10.00	$10.50
Hardware	Utility	5	2	1	0	12	8	$8.00	$7.75

Table 10-4. (continued)

Physical Demand	Mental Demand	Technical Demand	Leadership Demand
Pace	Grade/package	Interpret specifications	People skills/teamwork
Bending/twisting	Retention	Use measurement tools	Communication
Repetition	Repetition	Adjust machine	Initiative
Weight	Attention to detail	Develop and use setup criteria	Willing to be the example
Environment	Number of things to remember	Troubleshooting	Confidence
Endurance	Need to think ahead	Flexibility (multiple tasks)	Competence
Set the pace	Communication	Visualize (new product) process	Decision making, willingness/ability
	Paperwork accuracy	SPC charting	Training ability
	Quality awareness	Machine maintenance	Understanding material flow (integrated process requirements [RIP to ship])
	Safety awareness	Quality focus	Commitment
	Stacking patterns	Safety focus	Dedication to go the extra mile
		Ability to keep up visuals	Uphold company policy
		Willingness to participate	Ability to set quality expectations
		Willing to help	Ability to set safety expectations
		Accountability	Ability to create sense of urgency
			Self-motivated
			Focus on setup reduction
			Focus on productivity
			Can use the tools of TQM (kaizen) to problem solve
			Demonstrates high degree of urgency
			Acts as a resource and advocate for teammates

Table 10-4. (*continued*)

Wages			
Point Value	Scale	Point Value	Scale
1	7.75	32	10.50
2	7.75	33	10.50
3	7.75	34	11.75
4	7.75	35	11.75
5	7.75	36	11.75
6	7.75	37	11.75
7	7.75	38	11.75
8	7.75	39	11.75
9	7.75	40	12.25
10	7.75	41	12.25
11	7.75	42	12.25
12	7.75	43	12.25
13	8.50	44	12.25
14	8.50	45	12.25
15	8.50	46	12.25
16	8.50	47	12.25
17	8.50	48	12.75
18	8.50	49	12.75
19	8.50	50	12.75
20	9.75	51	12.75
21	9.75	52	12.75
22	9.75	53	12.75
23	9.75	54	13.25
24	9.75	55	13.25
25	9.75	56	13.25
26	9.75	57	13.25
27	10.50	58	13.25
28	10.50	59	13.25
29	10.50	60	13.25
30	10.50	61	13.25
31	10.50		

must be a measurable component related to ongoing machine reliability or overall equipment effectiveness.

The affect on quality must also be carefully monitored and measured. This program is not meant to emulate a piecework approach, but it has the potential of having people focus inordinately on productivity. We cannot afford to add so much to any one person's responsibility that he/she does not have time to focus adequate attention on the details of process control or quality requirements.

It is important to recognize both the positive and the negative impact of such sweeping changes. You may expect a period of time when the employees are so focused on making their jobs so demanding that they might take a cannibalistic attitude toward indirect labor or non-value-added personnel. This could create a positive effect on productivity, but negative effect on teamwork. It would obviously not be healthy for our team members to be at each other's throats, trying to eliminate each other's jobs. Some training early in the process would certainly help to prepare teams and individuals to think about utilizing normal attrition rather than layoffs as a means to remove non-value-added positions.

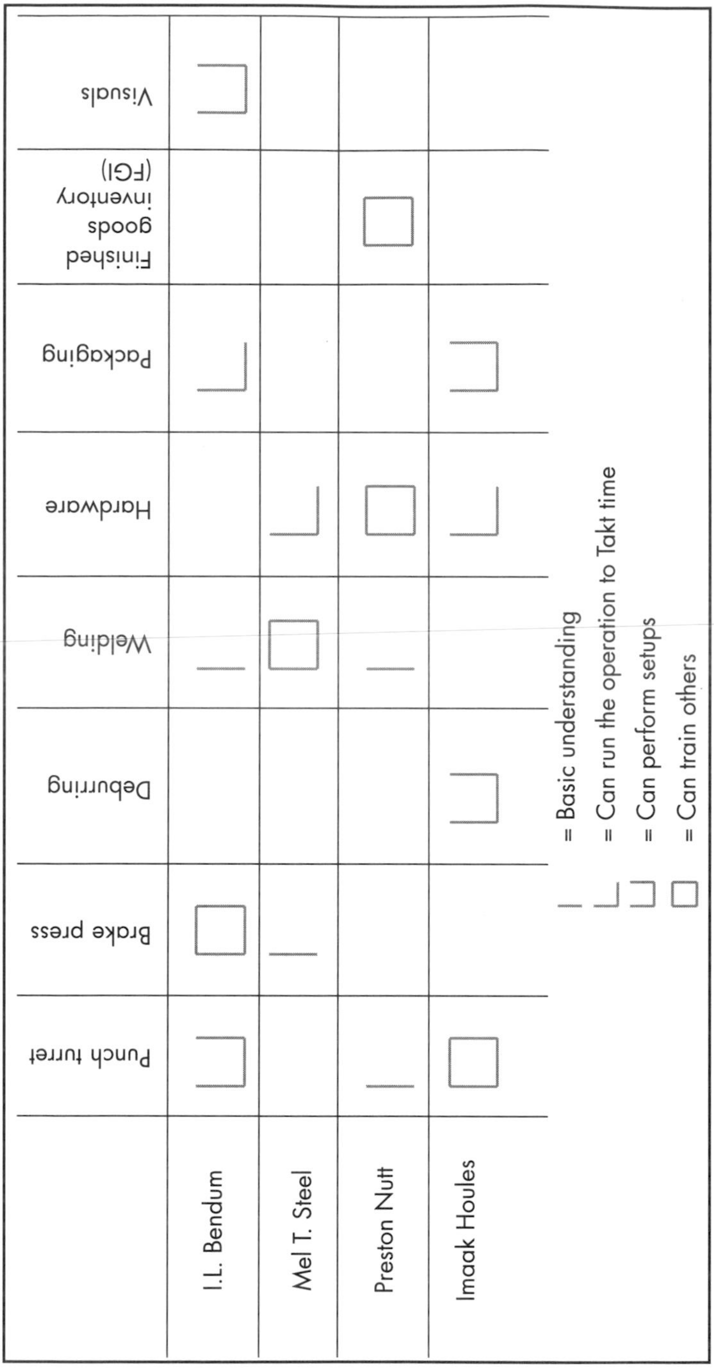

Figure 10-1. Cross-training matrix (depth chart) to identify skill levels.

Another possible solution is to utilize people freed up by productivity improvements to serve a role in the "Continuous Improvement Promotion Office."

Incentive Programs

In an earlier discussion about introducing and managing change, a point was made of the important role that incentive programs (or "what's in it for me?") play in a Lean transformation. The line is usually clearly drawn where people stand on the issue of gain-sharing or profit-sharing programs. People usually have a strong opinion one way or the other about the value that a company receives from offering such a program.

As mentioned earlier, money is not the only or even the primary driver for most people, but it is a driver. At some point an incentive program will be the only way to move from one productivity plateau to the next level.

Companies failing or struggling with such programs found that implementing them too late did not cause the greatest problem. It was more often the case that programs with marginal results were flawed because they were implemented too soon, while the company was still in a state of change, and the Lean processes were not yet stable.

Think about the benchmarks for paying an incentive as you would for any process that you are trying to control. We talked about Statistical Process Control (SPC) and process control in a previous chapter. When a process is unstable, it will do you little good to try to control it by using pre-control charts or other SPC tools. Just like driving on ice, you will end up oversteering and overbraking. In other words, you will overcontrol the process. A knee-jerk reaction to a positive or negative productivity measurement can have the company changing all the metrics related to the incentive program to avoid inordinate or non-existing funding of the program, only to see the results swing wildly in the opposite direction one or two months later. Soon no one trusts the system and what was meant to be an incentive becomes a source of discouragement and low morale.

It is much better to wait until the initial process of change is over and the system is stable. Even for small companies, this may take two or three years. This is not to say that incentives are not necessary. There are many forms of incentives that are not monetary. Team dinners, personal letters to employee's families recognizing exceptional effort, sincere praise, and time spent listening are all examples of incentives that can be used instead of financial rewards. There is also the option of one-time performance bonuses to help motivate teams to strive for the next level if they have hit a plateau.

Once you are ready for a gain-sharing program, don't try to set it up alone. A lot of these programs are designed over a couple of martinis and sketched out on the back of a bar napkin. It's no wonder that many of these efforts result in frustration. Get some help. There are experts available who can save you unbelievable amounts of time and money in the long run.

One consultant specialized in helping his clients set up incentive programs. One of the secrets to his success was a simple question he asked on the first day of a four-day workshop he held with the management team. After the usual greetings and introductions, he would stand, take a slow deliberate breath, and look at his wristwatch. Then, with an extremely serious look on his face, he would begin talking. "As a management team, you have a serious decision to make. Before we get going, you need to decide how much time you want to spend on this project."

He would then pause, continuing only after he had made eye contact with each person. "I can tell you that there are only two choices. We can do this over the course of the next four days. Or, we can be done here in four minutes."

Now the audience was wide-eyed with anticipation. How could this process take only four minutes when they were paying him thousands of dollars per day?

"The determining factor in deciding how long this project will last is in your answer to one question." Again he paused, letting the anxiety build.

"The question is this: Do you want to share? Because if you do want to share, this project is going to take us four days. If, on the other hand, you do not really want to share, then let's go play golf. You only owe me for four minutes work and a plane ticket home. We can all part as friends and it was very nice to meet you all."

Another pause, and then the question came again. "So, what'll it be? Do you want to share?" This time he waited for an answer.

If you are unwilling to share, you can't really expect anything above and beyond the ordinary from employees. Gain-sharing has been around long enough now that it can be categorized as a science. The cause and effect of a properly designed and implemented gain-sharing project is well documented and can be the catalyst for continued progress.

Here is an example of how a simple incentive program would look. Every company has unique realities that can and should affect how a program is designed. However, there are usually many key indicators within the control of the employees or teams. By focusing on these, they can pull together to impact the overall profitability in a positive way. Common measurements include: on-time delivery performance, productivity (labor hours per sales dollar), waste, quality claims as a percentage of sales, in-house rework as a percentage of sales, and variable spending (consumables, tooling, etc.).

By making the measurement realistic and the goal visible, people will focus on the cause and effect of their actions. They will begin to understand the value of everyone working together toward the same objectives, and over time they will begin to think more like business people.

While it is okay to experiment within the concept of a model line, be careful not to design a program that has multiple systems. This can cause division among teams and individuals. Team and individual performance can be better handled within a wage system. Everyone needs to see that the incentive or gain-sharing system is dependent on the success of the entire organization rather than sub-optimized departments. There is usually too much interdependency between all segments of a business to try building a gain-sharing program around each team. There could be a tendency to "cherry-pick" projects that make one department look good. The overall goal of becoming a Lean enterprise could never be met in such an internally competitive environment. On the other hand, one-time bonuses and other forms of incentives can be a tool for recognizing a team's extraordinary efforts or growth.

Figures 10-2 and 10-3 show how a gain-sharing program might be made visible and measurable.

Since world-class goals focus on improving quality, cost, and delivery performance, the "gain" in gain-share would only happen if the goals are changed to reflect the improvement objectives.

Most companies seeking the Lean approach focus on 20 percent productivity improvements per year (for the first five to six years). This seems like a lot, but it translates to 1.67 percent per month. It is not unusual for a company to recognize such amazing improvements the first few years after implementing Lean. However, there will come a time when the gains come slower. Over time, the annual productivity goal might be adjusted to five or 10 percent, or something more realistic. Remember that there is only so much low hanging fruit. Don't be so dogmatic about a goal that people get discouraged.

Teams need to understand that improvement is an expectation, and that the goals will be adjusted each month to ensure that the company is getting better. Otherwise there will be nothing to share.

One area of Figure 10-2 shows the employee share, which differs for each employee. In this example, the employee share is based first on a pre-determined level of profitability that the company must experience over the distribution period. It is also based on several other things: key performance criteria of the company, employee tenure with the company, and employee wages earned during the distribution period.

Figure 10-4 shows that the goals for the cost of supplies, productivity, on-time delivery, and quality have changed to reflect the improvement required this year. All the other data have remained the same. So without improvement, the financial result to the employee is marginal compared to the previous year. These goals cannot be changed arbitrarily; changes should support the goals outlined within the organizational vision statements.

Within a spreadsheet, the results can be simple to calculate and easily made visual by posting a daily, weekly, or monthly graph, as shown in Figure 10-3. The results show the entire workforce how their actions are having an impact on the gain-sharing system.

Monthly Gain-sharing Contribution (net profit/5)   **Total index points**   **22.81 (sum of net points)**

	Net Profit	Cont. x Index	Claims as a % of sales		Employees		
					Joe	Flo	Mo
Month 1	1,000.00	45.61	0%	Tenure points (# of years)	5	1	9
Month 2	800.00	36.49	1%	$500 Units of pay/period	18	16	22
Month 3	250.00	11.40	0%	Total # of participants	3	3	3
Month 4	-1,000.00	-45.61	2%	Total # of points to share	71	71	71
Month 5	300.00	13.68	0%	Per point value	1.64	1.64	1.64
Month 6	1,200.00	54.74	0%	Employee share	37.68	27.85	50.79
Total	2,550.00	116.32	0.5%				

	Gross Sales	Gross Margin %	Expenses	% On-time Deliveries	Quality Incentive	Labor per Sales $$	Yield %
Target	17,400	17	6,500	95.00	99.73	0.29	9
Actual	19,000	21	6,200	96.00	95.52	0.21	88
Under target multiplier	0.00	0.19	0.00	0.00	-0.96	0.00	-1.05
Over target multiplier	1.09	1.24	0.95	1.01	0.00	1.38	0.00
Weighted value	5	8	6	5	7	7	6
Net points	5.46	9.88	5.72	5.05	-6.70	9.67	-6.27

Jan	45.61	45.61
Feb	82.11	36.49
Mar	93.51	11.40
Apr	47.90	-45.61
May	51.58	13.68
June	115.32	54.74

Figure 10-2. Example gain-sharing program.

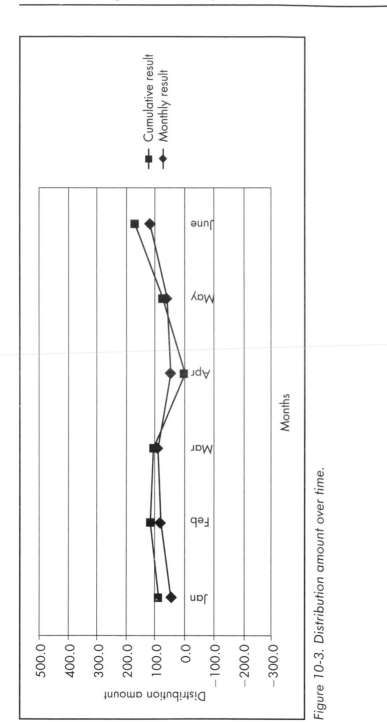

Figure 10-3. Distribution amount over time.

Monthly Gain-sharing Contribution (net profit/5)   Total index points   −1.45 (sum of net points)

	Net Profit	Cont. x Index	Claims as a % of sales			Employees		
						Joe	Flo	Mo
Month 1	1,000.00	−2.89	0%					
Month 2	800.00	−2.32	1%	Tenure points (# of years)		5	1	9
Month 3	250.00	−0.72	0%	$500 Units of pay/period		18	16	22
Month 4	−1,000.00	2.89	2%	Total # of participants		3	3	3
Month 5	300.00	−0.37	0%	Total # of points to share		71	71	71
Month 6	1,200.00	−3.47	0%	Per point value		−0.10	−0.10	−0.10
Total	2,550.00	−7.38	0.5%	Employee share		−2.39	−1.77	−3.22

	Gross Sales	Gross Margin %	Expenses	% On-time Deliveries	Quality Incentive	Labor per Sales $$	Yield %
Target	17,400	17	5,850	97.50	99.85	0.23	95
Actual	19,000	21	6,200	96.00	95.52	0.21	88
Under target multiplier	0.00	0.19	−1.06	−0.98	−0.96	0.00	−1.08
Over target multiplier	1.09	1.24	0.00	0.00	0.00	1.10	0.00
Weighted value	5	8	6	5	7	7	6
Net points	5.46	9.88	−6.36	−4.92	−6.70	7.67	−6.48

Jan	−2.89	−2.39
Feb	−2.32	−5.21
Mar	−0.72	−5.93
Apr	2.89	−3.04
May	−0.87	−3.91
June	−3.47	−7.38

Figure 10-4. Revised gain-sharing program for year two.

191

SUMMARY

People want to do a good job. It is human nature. We all want to be viewed as competent and capable. When given clear expectations, opportunity, and recognition, people will generally excel.

Personnel will not and cannot give 110 percent every day unless they feel that they are in business for themselves. Even business owners get discouraged at times, even though they may lose tens of thousands of dollars by not giving their all.

Humans are unique; we are all direction-oriented. At times we all need to locate our "true north," our seat of motivation. Money is certainly a motivator, but it has been shown not to be the ultimate motivator. Choice is the ultimate motivator. Until people understand and believe that they have a measure of control, they will tend to perform at the level they can get by with rather than to their greatest potential.

Give people "a choice and a voice" as to what their job descriptions and compensation packages will be, and they will often be much more demanding of themselves than any supervisor. There is a phrase in a country song, "Let the ponies run." If given the opportunity, employees allowed to feel like owner-operators will outperform your expectation. Management had better be prepared to let them run, or they could outrun management's ability to adapt.

11

Training

The growth in technology over the last few decades has been phenomenal. We have become so accustomed to change and improvement that when new technology is introduced, we may hardly take notice. There is danger in not taking notice. As business leaders and managers, we must stay sensitive to the way these changes affect those whom we employ and manage.

For example, many years ago, a company purchased a new piece of computer numerical control equipment. For the majority of shop personnel, it spawned two emotions: excitement and fear. The level of knowledge within the workforce at that time was such that no one was prepared to use the technology. It sat in a corner of the shop for about a week. No one wanted to be the first to fail or the first to damage this new machine. The owner's manuals sat on a table in front of the machine. Once in a while someone would sneak a peak at them, but no one was standing in line for a chance to run this new machine.

Finally, the company assigned someone to start using it. Although there were moments that this new technology looked to be a mistake, given enough time, the person was able to pour over the manual and grasp the concept of computer numeric controls as well as the new hydromechanical systems. Finally, after weeks, this new machine became a profitable investment for the company.

Today, that company would not have purchased the machine until it had either sent a few operators to a training program offered by the machine tool manufacturer, or until a representative had come to the facility to do on-site training.

There is a need to prepare people for success. We need to provide whatever training is necessary for them to succeed. Tool manufacturers, software, and systems design companies now regularly provide training as part of the purchase agreement when introducing new technologies. They realize how important skilled operators are in making the purchase of a machine profitable. The level of training can determine whether the day-to-day operation and use of machines, software, or new manufacturing technologies are effective or ineffective.

Technology is a wonderful thing. In its purest form we have seen it used in ways that bring gasps of disbelief. For example, in the medical field, technology has demonstrated its capacity to save lives. But all the technology in the world will not help if people are afraid to use it. Successful companies cannot rely on technology alone. They realize that the most critical part of the equation is the human element. Without the human component as part of the solution, even the most technological advances will fall short of desired goals. For example, what can technology do to build enthusiasm or create a sense of teamwork? How can technology provide the same sense of synergy experienced by the interaction of people on a high-performing team?

Methodologies such as cross-training, cellular manufacturing, and workload balancing are necessary if companies are to remain competitive. Yet, they are no different than any technology. These non-mechanical technologies of the Lean approach require a defined process and formal training programs if teams are to be effective.

It is through adequately trained personnel that our mission statements and goals will be attained. Technology, coupled with a clear understanding of how to utilize such advancements, allows personnel to do just that.

How can we prepare our employees to deal with increased demands of the marketplace as well as the constant technological changes in tools and methods of manufacturing or service? How can we ensure that our teams are capable of fully and successfully accomplishing their tasks in this new and competitive environment?

Training has generally been delegated to someone else. We send our kids to school, then we send them to college. If an employee needs training, we send him/her to a seminar or to a program of instruction at the local training center. We are in the habit of having someone else responsible for training. Granted, we are in business to make money. We are not in the business of training. However, if we are honest with ourselves, we know that as business managers we share some responsibility to provide training for our employees, not only so that they can be personally successful, but for the long-term benefit of our organizations.

TRAINING CONSIDERATIONS

In this section, we will discuss issues such as promoting from within the company; high-involvement training; how to train the trainers; trainer qualifications; and learning and communications styles.

Promoting from Within the Company

When we are looking for ways to train a greater pool of people in our operation or when we need to expand that pool due to increased production requirements, where does the greatest knowledge pool exist? Of course the answer is, within the walls of our own business.

It may have crossed your mind that if you could clone the individuals within your organization who have the highest level of skill and expertise, then you could duplicate the potential for increases in production, customer delivery, flexibility, and return on investment. Replicated skill within a greater pool of individuals has great potential for increased performance. Effective duplication of skill in multiple individuals is possible, if it is approached with the interests of all parties in mind. Identifying the parties involved is critical. There are three parties involved here:

1. The stakeholders—management must realize that there will be some cost involved in any training program. These costs will include time, costs, and effort on the part of the organization. The approach taken toward training must fit in with short- and long-term company goals.
2. The skilled person—the person or persons who have the knowledge necessary to accomplish the task must be considered. They must be approached in a manner that fosters trust and commitment to feel open to sharing their knowledge. Remember that it has taken them a lifetime to gain the knowledge that they hold. Willingness to share knowledge is a

learned behavior. Willingness is the key, and self-esteem is the key to willingness. You may find that when you are approached to train someone in a subject or skill that only you know something about, you may be uncomfortable until you know what the person plans to do with the information or skill. It is a human tendency to hold onto what we possess and no one else has. It gives us a sense of value and self-worth (however transitory). It is not easy to let that go when we see little or nothing there to replace it.

3. The person needing the skill—learning new skills can be difficult, and all the more so if training happens in a hostile or poorly structured environment. Learners deserve a safe environment within which they can feel free to ask, seek, fail, and grow, and at a rate at which they can adapt. These are separate and distinct needs that must be considered for each of the participants to feel a sense of accomplishment and fulfillment of purpose.

Trust and a strong value system are key to making a program like this work. If people feel that they are being manipulated to simply pump knowledge out of their head, or that sharing knowledge will make them less valued, the program will fail miserably, as would any program built on mistrust.

If, on the other hand, you show the benefits of cross-training and build trust through positive comments and actions, the program can become a self-perpetuating system of skill duplication and information sharing.

Because of stiff competition and fast moving technologies, no one has the luxury of enormous amounts of time. Just as technology has provided and driven us to new and faster forms of communication, it has just as surely driven us to find new and more effective ways of training others. If we are waiting for some easy fix or magic training pill to come along, we are going to get caught with our guard down.

High-involvement Training

Think back to the time when you first learned to ride a bicycle. Remember the moment when, after hours of trying, you realized you could stay up, pedal, and steer—all at the same time! Can you recapture the exhilaration of that moment? Can you see your face? Can you feel your heart pound? Can you hear the excitement in your voice as you described the sensation to your parents or best friend? Now hold onto that feeling for just a minute.

Imagine (or remember) a time when you teach your child, let's say your son, how to ride a two-wheeler. See the face of that child as you describe how you felt when you did it. Sense his confidence grow as you encourage him. Imagine his face as you describe what it will be like when he finally succeeds. Feel the roller coaster of his emotion as you run along side, holding on first to steady him, then just for moral support.

Finally, there comes the moment when you have to let go. You've taught him all you can. Your heart pounds again, but now it pounds for him. You are conscious that he has to do the rest for himself. Your hand separates from the seat. He is not yet aware that he is on his own. Now, you live the roller coaster ride between exhilaration and terror as he falters and wobbles. Finally, he crosses that fine line between balance and imbalance. The distance between you grows. Then, the moment he looks back, it takes your breath away. Surprised to find himself on his own, he realizes that he has done it; he learned! You realize that you have done it, also. Think about the accomplishment of this simple story, someone who taught, someone who learned, and both are more valued because of the experience. That is what *high-involvement training* is all about. Once people have experienced the satisfaction that teaching others brings, it is hard to replace that feeling with any other. It is an experience that makes us whole.

As humans, we do well to realize that we cannot be complete if we do not share. We must be able to give of ourselves to receive a sense of self-value, to feel that others have benefited from our being here.

For a structured training program to be truly effective, there must be a level of trust inherent in the system to demonstrate to the ones training that, once they train others to know what they know, not only will they still be valued, but even more so.

We must foster an environment that values the willingness and ability to share knowledge as much as the ability to carry out day-to-day operational activities. If we do this, if we can show all the team members within our organization that it is safe and beneficial to train others to do their job, then we will be well under way toward gaining the trust necessary to implement a world-class training system.

Training the Trainers

Don't be too quick to count out a skill as untrainable in-house. Survey your work force to see what skills are hidden within the ranks of the team. One company was sending people off to a college math class, 65 miles round trip, when they found that one of their other employees was just a few credit hours away from a master's degree in mathematics. They are now offering his classes in-house and everyone is benefiting from his previously hidden talents.

Once you have developed a list of trainable and measurable skills, find persons within the company who can provide the most complete overview for that particular operation. Sit down with them and record their knowledge on paper. You will, of course, need to define how many distinct types of operations there are and how many skill categories (levels) there are within each operation. It may take many sessions to identify and document all the skills needed in each operation. In this process, you are trying to write down as much as possible of what the expert knows. Table 11-1 gives some key points for discussion during such an interview.

When developing the training assessment outline for measuring training effectiveness, think about the following questions:

1. Is the objective clearly stated, and will the trainee understand what skills will be measured at the end of the training cycle?
2. Does the assessment description clearly explain the task or criteria by which the knowledge of the trainee will be measured?
3. Does the assessment criteria define the lower limit of acceptability so that the training program can meet these needs and thus prepare the trainee for an evaluation?

By keeping these questions in mind, you should be able to develop a clear and concise training assessment outline that will prove beneficial to trainer and trainee alike.

Table 11-1. Training interview list

Department:_____ Interviewee: _____

Machine ID:_____ Interviewer: _____

Variations of machine: _____

Hand tools: _____

Measurement tools:_____

Math requirements:_____

Safety concerns:_____

Specifications/documentation: _____

Materials:_____

Tooling (location, storage, handling, load/unload):_____

Quality requirements and concerns: _____

Equipment nomenclature: _____

Machine adjustments:_____

Basic skills (first day): _____

Machine start-up and shut down: _____

Standard work: _____

Secondary skills (first week): _____

Advanced skills (first month): _____

Basic setup skills: _____

Advanced setup skills:_____

Horror stories:_____

Trainer Qualifications

What qualifications should you look for in an individual whom you would select to train others? First and foremost, the person must be humble. Effective training requires the trainer to put himself or herself in the position of the learner. Those who cannot demonstrate empathy and care do not make good trainers.

The learning process is a delicate one. It requires humility to admit that you do not know something. In doing this, you put yourself in an emotionally vulnerable position. Thus, it requires a high level of empathy on the part of the instructor when providing the required new information. Maybe you have lived through the pain of watching a knowledgeable but unfeeling person try to transfer knowledge to someone else. Displays by the trainer of frustration, sarcasm, or lack of patience will stifle the ability of the learner to absorb or mentally process the information. If the training process is geared toward the needs of the trainer instead of the trainee, the chances are high that both will go away frustrated and possibly angry. It makes very little difference how much a trainer knows. It is more important that the trainer can empathize and care about the trainee's needs.

Second, the person delivering the material must communicate clearly and check for understanding. Checking for understanding means stopping and asking viewpoint questions, then watching and listening for expressions that demonstrate knowledge and agreement. There is a need to be sensitive to the fact that not everyone will ask for clarifying information. Effective trainers listen attentively to questions asked by the person being trained and they watch for body language that indicates questions or confusion.

Adult versus Child Learners

It is important to realize that adult learners are different from child learners. In school, our teachers told us what they wanted us to know and we then had to tell them what they told us. We did not question the value of the information.

In the adult learning environment, you first must give the learner clear evidence of why it is important to them to learn the information.

As busy adults we have a lot of input every day, and so we become selective listeners. We generally choose to listen only to what we consider to be of value. Have the first part of your outline include the benefits and reasons to listen.

Communication Styles

We have all experienced being in a seminar or class where the instructor was a poor communicator. The learning process is difficult enough without the added problem of poor communication or an inadequate style of delivery.

You need to understand the communication style of others. The trainer has the responsibility to adapt his or her presentation style to meet the needs of the learner. For example, an instructor was struggling with giving information to students from Romania who were limited in their ability to speak English. They were technologically trained very well. They were in the class to learn the English equivalent for the technical terms they needed to apply their skills and obtain employment in the United States. The instructor's friend was able to describe the many ways in which people prefer to communicate.

First, he drew a dot about the size of a silver dollar on the white board and said, "This dot represents something that I want you to know." He then connected an arrow to it and added, "This is the way most Americans prefer to communicate. We are fairly direct in our communication style. You might say we aim right at it!" (see Figure 11-1.)

He then drew another dot and explained that if he were of Japanese descent he would probably prefer to communicate differently. He added a number of smaller dots surrounding the first larger dot, as shown in Figure 11-2. He went on to explain, "These small dots represent ideas related to the larger dot. Because the Japanese culture allows you to draw conclusions for yourself rather than me telling you outright what I want

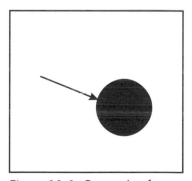

Figure 11-1. One style of communication.

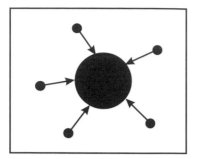

Figure 11-2. Another style of communication.

you to know, I will not be as direct with you as someone raised in the American culture.

"To us, this style seems to lack direction. It feels fragmented and hard to understand. However, to the Japanese our style seems too direct, even abrasive. It is viewed as an affront to explain the main point under discussion and not allow people to reach the conclusion on their own. You can begin to see how the two communication styles can conflict with each other. It's no wonder that our two cultures don't communicate at times."

To illustrate yet another communication style, he drew two more dots on the board, as shown in Figure 11-3. This time he connected an arrow to each dot. The two arrow lines were parallel to each other. Again he pointed to one of the dots (the dark one) and explained that it represented something he wanted the instructor to know. Then, while pointing to the lighter dot, he went on to explain, "If I were of Jewish or Native American descent, I would likely choose to communicate with you this way, because their societies place high value on biblical accounts or ancestral stories to prove a point. This leads them to speak (and listen) most effectively using parallel lines of communication. In other words, if a person of this communication style wanted you to know something, he might tell you a story that leads you to the moral or conclusion that he wants you to reach. As a trainee, that is how he is conditioned to listen. He might not 'get it' until you use an illustration or example." These are just a few of the examples. The point in sharing this is to highlight the need to select trainers who care about meeting the needs of others.

Though there are many styles, there is no "right way" or "wrong style" of communication. There are

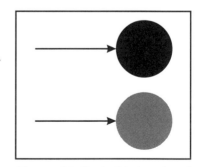

Figure 11-3. A third style of communication.

simply differences. Think what you would do if you were training a blind or a deaf person. You would certainly need to modify your approach to meet the unique training needs of the person. It is the same with any group of trainees. Gear your presentation to fit the needs of your audience and you will always be more effective. This is a learned behavior for most of us. "Train the trainer" courses available at most community colleges are a great place to help potential trainers develop the skills they will need.

It may be that the trainees learn best by seeing, so have some samples and examples. Possibly they prefer hearing new information, so give some lecture. For others, reading is preferred, so provide handouts for them to take home. In some cases, performing or practicing the new skill helps to "lock in" on the new information. Others need to see the new skill demonstrated a number of times to develop a mental list of "how it is done."

Make sure that trainers pay attention to every possible learning style. This may cause some repetition to cover multiple learning styles, but repetition will serve all learners well. The old saying is true: "Repetition is the mother of retention."

If the trainees don't know anything about learning styles, help them to understand that they each have preferred styles. When they recognize that the trainer is sensitive to their individual needs, it will actually help them pay closer attention.

It has been said that if you just stand and lecture to someone about a new subject, the trainees will retain about 10 percent of what you say. If you have visual aids, they will increase their retention to between 30 and 40 percent. If you allow them to perform the new skill or demonstrate the new skill or knowledge, they will retain about 60 percent. That's about as good as it gets, unless you use a technique called "teach back."

Teach Back

The *teach back* method requires the trainee to recall and demonstrate the just-learned skill or subject. For example, if I were to ask you to read this chapter, you would probably pay some measure of attention. If, on the other hand, I asked you to read this chapter and then give a book review to a group of people, you would no doubt read it quite differently. You would pay more attention to the key information. This is the principle behind the teach back method. If you let the students know (prior to training) how they will be measured, and if the measurement includes teaching back or demonstrating knowledge about the new skill, their learning process will be most effective.

SUMMARY

In summary, we must take responsibility for training our people. The ISO 9000 structure addresses this requirement. It is not easy, but if you effectively implement a system that allows people a choice, the self-esteem of your employees will be enhanced, as will your company's profit and loss statement.

Most managers have had the benefit of someone to help guide them in their career path, perhaps a high school counselor, a college professor, a parent, or a mentor. Not all hourly employees have had the privilege of such guidance. We can help provide a measure of such direction. An effective training program can provide the guideposts for people as they become better at controlling their own destiny.

12

Team Structure for the 21st Century

High-involvement training, enfranchised business units . . . are we asking too much of teams? Like raising kids, the answer depends a lot on the kids. Some children mature faster and can accept and even seek more responsibility. Other children are quite happy to let mom and dad make all the decisions. If you push them too fast, they will often suffer the effects of stress and anxiety.

When you have a team of high performers, pushing toward accepting more responsibility will work well. When the group tends to wait for direction on every minor decision or improvement opportunity, it will take longer.

Table 12-1 shows a tool you can use to assist teams in moving forward. This tool is called a *team enfranchisement continuum*. Notice that in the top part of the continuum, the text is placed vertically. This area shows the level of responsibility for decision-making changes over time as the team matures (from left to right). This growth is evidenced by the performance of the team shown in the lower part of the continuum. For example, a team that is not yet using standard work or not utilizing fast setup technologies may not have demonstrated the maturity to manage their own tooling budget.

TOOLS FOR IMPROVING THE TEAM

We will now discuss how peer-to-peer evaluations and determining potential leaders will improve productivity.

Peer-to-peer Evaluations

One of the most powerful tools that a team can use to speed the maturing process is to offer feedback to each other. But without

Table 12-1. Team enfranchisement continuum

Supervisor Led ——————————————————→ Team Led

Supervisor decides	Supervisor presents decision, asks for input	Supervisor presents the situation and asks employees for ideas, then supervisor makes a decision	Supervisor allows team to experiment, then offers feedback and recommends alternatives	Team handles daily productivity and quality issues; leader handles personnel functions	Leader shares expertise in personnel function areas while transferring other functions to the team	Team is self-sufficient; leader consults as needed and spends more time on strategic issues
Takt times are known and visible	High degree of focus placed on reducing setup times	Team demonstrates some self-sufficiency	Team performs most preventive maintenance (PM) activities	Supermarkets are in place for key product types	Paperless systems are in place for key products	Team manages their own tooling budget
Best practices and setup sheets are used	Team operates within a culture of continuous improvement	Team develops future state map	Team projects focus on elimination of process variation	Team manages visual measurements	Team performs its own world-class training	50% of all paperwork orders have been eliminated
Team meets regularly to discuss improvements	Team maintains and implements standard work	Team develops tailored rules of engagement for team operation	Model line pull signals are implemented on a trial basis	Team manages uptime and crewing levels	Team performs basic HR functions	Team performs one kaizen event per month (formal or informal)
Team understands and works toward one-piece flow	Visuals are in place and maintained	Provides vehicle for customer feedback	Consistent setup times are less than 10 min average	Scheduling is built into team responsibilities	Team manages overtime schedules	Team does its own hiring
Team experiments with pull systems	5-S is used to organize work areas	Practices paperwork reduction	Operator cycle time is equal to takt time and is balanced	Assists with new product introduction	Team manages variable spending (with assistance)	Team performs most purchasing functions
Team discusses its strengths and weaknesses	Supplier feedback systems are used	Plans and participates in at least one kaizen event per quarter	Team manages rework and recovery labor	Team reps. participate in interview process for potential new members	Team participates in some hiring decisions	Team develops its own vacation schedule
Develops team mission statement	Lean principles are understood by all team members	Training depth chart is used to ensure skill base is adequate	Team conducts some of its own kaizen events	Team conducts all of its kaizen events	Team acts as model for other teams; teaches others continuous improvement (CI) program	

proper training, this can be more destructive than useful. In school, they teach math, reading, and science, but seldom do they teach teams how to grow together or how to build an effective business unit together. Feedback has been called the "breakfast of champions." There are two kinds of feedback: positive and corrective.

Positive feedback is easy to receive. Corrective feedback takes a bit more effort to offer or to receive. In either case, for feedback is to be effective, it must be specific and sincere. The one receiving the feedback must feel that the one offering the feedback has his/ her best interest at heart.

Table 12-2 shows a tool that teams can use to offer feedback about critical team responsibilities. When offered in the spirit of continuous improvement, and without sharing the individual results with the entire team, people will usually welcome the opportunity to know how the team views their strengths and opportunities. Notice that I did not use the term "weakness." A lack of strength is merely an opportunity.

The power of this tool is that it is anonymous and each team member has the chance to offer feedback to each of the other members. Where there is a gap, the person finds out anonymously and can work on that opportunity. When the team sees the effort, both can feel good that they had a part to play in the personal growth of the individual as well as the team. The results of this needs to be shared with each individual, not in front of the group. Focus on the strengths as well as the opportunities. Do not compare individuals. Instead, compare against the team average, as shown in Table 12-3.

Determining a Leader

Let's talk about team leadership. This is a mixed bag. We would like to think that the team could be self-managing, but at times, particularly in the early stages of team development, it is important to identify someone who will be charged with certain responsibilities. How can a leader be selected, whom the team can fully support, and in whom the management team can have full confidence? If the team votes, the selection may be little more than a personality contest. If management appoints someone, the team may bristle at the thought of having no voice in the process.

Table 12-2. Peer-to-peer evaluation worksheet

Characteristic	Ted	Fred	Ned	Jed	Achmed	Red	Barney	Team Average
Positive attitude	3.5	3.1	3.6	3.0	3.1	2.7	3.3	3.2
Self-motivated	3.8	3.3	3.6	3.0	3.0	3.0	3.4	3.3
Open to new ideas	3.8	3.5	3.8	3.3	3.3	2.8	3.7	3.5
Willing to help out	3.6	3.5	3.8	2.9	3.2	3.2	3.5	3.4
Communicates well	3.8	3.3	3.7	2.9	2.8	2.8	3.3	3.2
Dependable	4.3	2.9	3.2	3.8	3.8	3.3	4.0	3.6
Organized	3.8	3.5	3.4	3.1	3.1	3.0	3.5	3.3
Wants to win	3.7	3.4	3.7	3.3	3.3	3.7	3.6	3.5
Team player	3.9	3.8	3.8	3.3	3.3	3.3	3.9	3.6
Team average	3.8	3.4	3.6	3.2	3.2	3.1	3.6	3.4

Table 12-3. Peer-to-peer evaluation worksheet showing feedback to employee

Characteristic	Ted	Fred	Ned	Jed	Achmed	Red	Barney	Team Average
Positive attitude			3.6					3.2
Self-motivated			3.6					3.3
Open to new ideas			3.8					3.5
Willing to help out			3.8					3.4
Communicates well			3.7					3.2
Dependable			3.2					3.6
Organized			3.4					3.3
Wants to win			3.7					3.5
Team player			3.8					3.6
Team average			3.6					3.4

The following is a nearly flawless approach to reaching consensus among team members, while satisfying the needs for management's confidence that adequate leadership is in place.

Start the process by gathering the group together around a flip chart, asking them to freely express themselves to each question asked. Depending on the group, you may choose to not yet inform them that they are gathered together to decide who will lead the team.

Draw two vertical lines on the flip chart, dividing the paper into three equal parts (you could use a white board). The first question is this: "Who were the greatest leaders in history?" Without exception, the list will always include names such as those shown in Figure 12-1. List all the names that the team suggests. If they do not list Jesus Christ, General George Patton, or Napoleon Bonaparte, then ask if you may add them.

Then, using the second column, take the team back through the list of names, asking what were the outstanding characteristics of each person that made him or her a great leader, as shown in Figures 12-2 and 12-3. Do not write a novel about each person. Try to reduce it to a one-word description of what set this person apart from other leaders.

Next, go back through the list one more time, this time attaching a numerical value to each characteristic. This is when you usually introduce them to the idea that, together, you would like to formulate a recommendation to management about who should lead the team. The scoring process involves simply having the team express how important it would be for their team leader to be able to demonstrate the characteristic under discussion. Each characteristic will have one number assigned to it. The number should be an average of what people call out. Don't make this complicated. Just ask the group to shout out a number between one and five to show how critical they consider each characteristic. If three people say honesty should rate a four, and three other people say it should rate a five, average it in your head, and ask the group if recording 4.5 would be okay. Allow them some time to talk about each value, but do not belabor the process. The entire process should take less than 15 minutes.

The last step is to find out who among the team wants to be considered for the team leader. It is okay for the management team

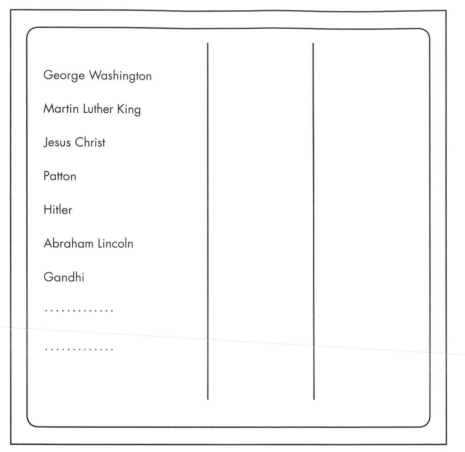

George Washington

Martin Luther King

Jesus Christ

Patton

Hitler

Abraham Lincoln

Gandhi

. . . .

. . . .

Figure 12-1. First step in the team leader selection process: listing names of the great leaders in history.

to make a suggestion as well. A little discussion with the team about how this process works would be in order at this time. They need to understand that their recommendation has to be strictly a business decision. Personalities, loyalties, prejudices, or relationships can have no part in the decision.

Each person wishing to be considered should have his/her name attached to the top of a form such as the one shown in Table 12-4. Each team member should then be given time (maybe overnight) to take the list and rate each person's demonstrated ability to manifest the characteristics judged to be important in a leader. To

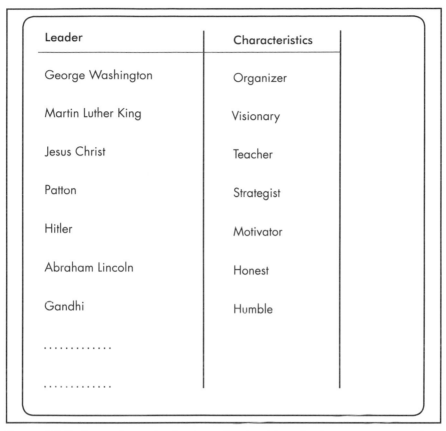

Leader	Characteristics
George Washington	Organizer
Martin Luther King	Visionary
Jesus Christ	Teacher
Patton	Strategist
Hitler	Motivator
Abraham Lincoln	Honest
Gandhi	Humble
. . . .	
. . . .	

Figure 12-2. Second step in the team leadership selection process: naming the outstanding characteristics of historic leaders.

have reasonable results, each person is given the same instructions about scoring. Multiply the number of candidates by two (in this case 3 candidates × 2 = 6).

Each characteristic is scored separately. You can assign up to six points total, but no more than one-half of the points can be given to any one person. Notice that none of the scores in Table 12-4 are over three, and no characteristic has been assigned more than six points. However, you can assign less than the total six points. Notice the first example, visionary, was only assigned four points total. Evidently, none of the candidates have demonstrated strength in this area.

Leader	Characteristics	Value
George Washington	Organizer	3.5
Martin Luther King	Visionary	4
Jesus Christ	Teacher	3
Patton	Strategist	3
Hitler	Motivator	4
Abraham Lincoln	Honest	4.5
Gandhi	Humble	3
. . . .		
. . . .		

Figure 12-3. Third step in the team leadership selection process: assigning a value to the leadership characteristics.

Once all the scores are assigned, the sheets can be turned over to the facilitator to tabulate. This can take some time, so it often works best to do this between meetings. Each score is multiplied against the value placed on the characteristic. This avoids having the same weight applied to a low-importance behavior as a critically needed characteristic. The results of this multiplication process are shown in Table 12-5. The total result is posted on the bottom of the table and should help make the selection a no-brainer. If there are very close scores between two candidates, the team may opt to repeat the process for the standout candi-

Table 12-4. Team leadership selection worksheet 1

Characteristic	Value	Joe	Flo	Mo
Visionary	4.5	1	2	1
Mediator (negotiator)	5	2	3	1
Strategist/organizer	5	1	3	2
Teacher	5	2	3	1
Humanitarian/cares about people	5	2	2	1
Honesty	5	2	2	2
Well disciplined (positively)	5	2	1	2
Motivator	4	2	2	1
Good head for numbers	4.5	1	3	2
Communicator	5	2	3	1
Technical skills	5	1	2	3
Self-motivated	4.5	1	2	3
Fair	5	2	3	1
Good listener	4.5	2	3	1
Product and process knowledge	4	1	2	3
Positive attitude	5	3	2	1
Consistent temperament	3	3	2	1

dates, or choose to have co-leaders, or have leadership that rotates on a monthly basis.

Each candidate should see the results against the average rather than against another candidate, as shown in Table 12-6. Where there is a need to grow in an area of opportunity, the person can focus on this in preparation for the next time a leadership position is available. This becomes a very powerful tool to coach individuals and teams.

The same process can work to assist teams to develop strong feedback capability. Teams often struggle with peer-to-peer feedback and evaluation. Most often feedback manifests itself in the form of pent-up frustration or an explosion of emotion.

One more question needs to be asked of every individual on the team: "This selection may or may not have been your first choice. However, can you support the recommendation of this person as

Table 12-5. Team leadership selection worksheet 2

Characteristic	Value	Joe	Flo	Mo
Visionary	4.5	4.5	9	4.5
Mediator (negotiator)	5	10	15	5
Strategist/organizer	5	5	15	10
Teacher	5	10	15	5
Humanitarian/cares about people	5	10	10	5
Honesty	5	10	10	10
Well disciplined (positively)	5	10	5	10
Motivator	4	8	8	4
Good head for numbers	4.5	4.5	13.5	9
Communicator	5	10	15	5
Technical skills	5	5	10	15
Self-motivated	4.5	4.5	9	13.5
Fair	5	10	15	5
Good listener	4.5	9	13.5	4.5
Wood product experience	4	4	8	12
Positive attitude	5	15	10	5
Consistent temperament	3	9	6	3
Totals		138.5	187	125.5

your team leader?" Each person should be asked to vocalize his or her support for the recommendation. Change is difficult, no matter how effective the vehicle used to introduce it. Without this expression of support in front of the peer group, there still might be the tendency of some to second-guess the selection.

It may still fall to the management team to make a final decision. But rarely will a group using this process come up with a person different from who the management team would select (assuming they both had the same list of people).

SUMMARY

Group dynamics are an issue that every manager should study. Manage the human resource as well as you manage the material, machines, customer relations, and capital. The results can only be positive.

Table 12-6. Team leadership selection worksheet 3

Characteristic	Value	Joe	Average
Visionary	4.5	4.5	6
Mediator (negotiator)	5	10	10
Strategist/organizer	5	5	10
Teacher	5	10	10
Humanitarian/cares about people	5	10	8.3
Honesty	5	10	10
Well disciplined (positively)	5	10	8.3
Motivator	4	8	6.7
Good head for numbers	4.5	4.5	9
Communicator	5	10	10
Technical skills	5	5	10
Self-motivated	4.5	4.5	9
Fair	5	10	10
Good listener	4.5	9	9
Wood product experience	4	4	8
Positive attitude	5	15	10
Consistent temperament	3	9	6
Totals		138.5	150.3

13

The Road to Lean

How many times have I used the term "model line" in this book? Without a real-life example, it will be hard to demonstrate or convince the chief executive officer (CEO), chief financial officer (CFO), vice-president of operations, shareholders, customers, vendors, the manufacturing leadership, or even the hourly employees that there are financial, quality, lead time, and morale improvements possible from using the Lean approach.

If you play golf or tennis, there comes a time when your game hits a plateau. Without some coaching, improvement will be slow. The answer is often to hire a professional—a "pro"—to watch you and offer feedback. It is also beneficial to watch other people play. You can pick up subtle actions that you can incorporate into your own style.

In sports or hobbies, no one looks down on you when you hire a pro, or when you admit that you need help. In fact, they respect your desire to improve. Yet, in business, people are often more reserved about asking for help. Maybe they are afraid people will be upset if they do not have all the answers. Or, maybe they "don't know what they don't know" and are just blind to the fact that they need help. A model line can assist in overcoming some of the trepidation about asking for help. It is an experiment and no one has all the answers in an experiment.

The value and benefits of developing a model line make a long list. The model line gives you a chance to try out new technologies without disrupting the entire plant. It allows you to measure the effect without the complexity of all the variables introduced by the rest of the operation. It avoids the "mile wide, inch deep" trap that some companies experience. Therefore the efforts are not diluted.

Another benefit is the "fishbowl" effect, a chance for the team operating the model line to experience a heightened sense of participation and prominence in the company. There is an equal chance for other teams to view this attention as a negative, so be careful to manage the morale of all employees. The team is generally allowed a wide range of new responsibilities and the rest of the employees are able to see the morale, camaraderie, and cohesiveness that can quickly develop when a team is offered a chance to work toward a defined set of measurable objectives. The list goes on and on.

The performance of a model line can be the catalyst for moving the company forward. This is why it is so critical to select the right project, the right team, the right equipment, and the right set of part numbers when beginning this process. Recovering from a failure early in the transformation period can be very difficult. This is not meant to sound negative. The message is simply that if there are potential pitfalls, we should make every effort to avoid them. On the other hand, don't pick a project that is a no-brainer. There is not much satisfaction in a project that is for show only. Choose a project that is meaningful, important to the future of the company, and has a fair chance of success if the team works hard at it.

One of the most important steps in selecting a model line is to "go where the energy is." It is very difficult to push water uphill. Just about the time you think you've got it, it runs back down, and you have to start all over. Trying to push someone along in this transformation can work in a mature Lean environment, but it can be fatal to a program in the early stages if the person(s) responsible for implementation does not believe in the process. Find the energy in the organization and plug into it. Find the people who are readers and communicators, who are not territorial, who are not mental dinosaurs, who listen to other people, those who are always coming to you with wild ideas.

People who are energetic sometimes have other personality traits that make you uncomfortable. They often do not (or choose not to) understand the word "can't." They ask too many questions. They can be flighty. They can have the entrepreneurial spirit, always dreaming of foolish things like starting their own business. They are always busy, at work and away from work. Their desks are messy. They borrow tools and rarely bring them back because they are onto new projects before cleaning up from the last one. They are always talking about some "big deal" they are working on. You may never be fully confident that they will be around next month or next year. However, the benefits of having people like this around outweigh the drawbacks. If you can challenge them by providing a chance to participate in something new, they will work extremely hard at making it a success. Tap into their energy for as long as you have access to it. If they leave to go try out some idea, don't feel bad about it. Tell them to come back. While they are gone, they will gain more experience that you can tap into when they return.

There are good and bad aspects of surrounding yourself with energetic people. Like a spirited horse, they will not be easily tamed. Don't try to overcontrol them, but find a way to harness the power of their creativity and their intensity. Harnessing this energy is a challenge, but the rewards of selecting the right team are obvious and critical.

One book on the subject of human nature describes the dynamics of four primary personality styles and how they each react and interact with each other. For me, the message in the book was that by understanding each personality style, and capitalizing on the differences, a team could be a lot stronger by having diversity (more than one kind of personality) in the group. The differences can cause a team to struggle at times. But if team members are trained to understand how their differences enhance the team's potential, they can avoid many problems and become a much higher-performing team than those where there is little diversity.

A word of warning: use the team development continuum (Chapter 12, Table 12-1) to guide you in determining how quickly to transfer decision-making responsibility to the team. If you have children, think about parents turning over the car keys on the day their child turns 16 years old. To over-empower a youngster can have long-lasting negative effects. Over-enfranchised teams, if given excessive responsibility with little or no boundaries, can be as ineffective and potentially dangerous to a program as an untrained teenage driver.

Teams operating in a model line need to understand their role. They also need to understand the role of management. A list of accountabilities and responsibilities as listed in the roadmap given in this chapter can help teams and organizations focus on very specific and defined goals.

Too often, direction is left to chance. People are left to wonder about their roles and responsibilities. Like doing the dishes at home, if it's everybody's job, then it's nobody's job.

ADOPTING THE LEAN APPROACH

The overall goal is to significantly improve the manufacturing performance and competitive posture of the company. For the Lean approach to succeed, a solid plan that states the vision and defines objectives and strategies must be devised.

Vision Statement

To begin, a vision statement must be developed, upon which the strategies and objectives for adopting the Lean approach can be built. Creating a vision statement will help "The Jobbe Shoppe's" entire team aim for and hit the target objectives that the company has identified as critical. It will also assist them in following through on their responsibilities to each other.

Broad Objectives

- Foster a commitment to continuous improvement with increased visibility of how we use time. Reduce or eliminate activities that do not add value.
- Foster a commitment to a high level of quality—doing the right things right the first time.
- Apply state-of-the-art tools for waste reduction and quality improvement.
- Change the management culture from "traditional" to "team oriented," enhancing employee involvement at all levels.
- Employ statistical management techniques as a new language for all employees, identifying problems when they occur, and resolving them at the lowest possible level in the organization.
- Train employees to be team leaders, facilitators, and team members in accordance with the new culture.

- Foster innovation and commitment to being world class at all levels.
- Promote the use of consensus decision-making whenever possible as the foundation for the new culture.
- Support these objectives with data collection and accounting procedures that focus on critical "cost drivers."

First Year Objectives

- Identify and carry out pilot projects including a physical "model line" that uses Just-in-Time/Total Quality Management principles.
- Document cost savings associated with the pilot projects and model line equal to or greater than cost.
- Enhance the management teams' commitment to continuous improvement.
- Lay the groundwork for expanded application of productivity and quality improvement tools and techniques.

Market Imperatives

- Compress lead-time from six weeks to two weeks.
- Improve on-time delivery performance from 75 to 95 percent.

Current Conditions

Backlog: 2–3 weeks (shippable orders)
Setup times: punch, 45 minutes
               brake, 40 minutes
               hardware, 30 minutes
               spot weld, 25 minutes
Material management: batch-push
Subcontract lead times: 1–2 weeks
Lot sizes: 90 days
Inventory turns: 8 turns/year
Lead time: 5–8 weeks (including outside processes)
Facilities layout: process functional, multiple buildings
Quality: Cost = 2% of sales
Productivity: $85K per employee/year ($120K direct labor)

To-be Vision

Backlog: 3 days maximum (shippable orders)
Setup times: punch, 9 minutes
               brake, 12 minutes
               hardware, 5 minutes
               spot weld, 9 minutes
Material management: demand pull
Subcontract lead times: 2–3 days
Lot sizes: 2 weeks
Inventory turns: 20 turns/year
Lead time: 9–11 days (including outside processes)
Facilities layout: cellular, single building
Quality: cost < 1% of sales
Productivity: $100K per employee/year ($130K direct labor)

Model-line personnel will exhibit the following characteristics:

- Accept only zero quality rejections;
- Are not passive witnesses;
- Keep the flow;
- Continually suggest improvement;
- Are interested in production goals;
- Know how to do their jobs;
- Know how to do others' jobs;
- Can stop the line;
- Assist their teammates;
- Predict and avoid problems;
- Measure their own output;
- Measure their own quality;
- Understand the product;
- Understand the process;
- Call in resources as needed;
- Communicate, cooperate, collaborate; and
- Are team players and team leaders.

Program Organization

To develop a plan for making an organization lean, the roles of the steering team, continuous improvement coordinator, model-line team leader, model-line team members, managers, and supervisors, should be defined. Also, the project scope and structure, criteria for team member selection, consensus decision making, and presentations should be discussed.

Role of the Steering Team

The steering team's responsibility is to create a vision statement and make sure the Lean process doesn't get off track. It is also responsible for communication, behavior modeling, collaboration, and team management and support. A list of duties includes:

- Visits other successful companies;
- Provides organizational development through training;
- Generates, revises, maintains the vision;
- Develops and communicates the vision and plan, formally and informally;
- Acts as strong sponsor for the entire improvement process;
- Remains visible in the implementation process;
- Sets the example (good at the fundamentals);
- Demonstrates the new values of absolute quality and waste elimination;
- Models pro-active behavior;
- Begins and ends meetings on time;
- Uses consensus decision-making;
- Supports "do it right the first time";
- Directs, informs, and guides the continuous improvement coordinator, outside consultants, and model-line team in a collaborative manner;
- Resolves disagreement by consensus;
- Meets periodically (not less than monthly) to review the progress of the program;
- Encourages and sponsors program activities and strongly sponsors the successful adaptation of the new philosophy at The Jobbe Shoppe;
- Chooses problem/opportunity areas for teams to work on;
- Creates guidelines and provides support to team (for example, defines boundaries, expectations);
- Meets with team leaders and program coordinator to review problem statement, milestones, and action plans;

- Manages change by spreading and demonstrating (by action) the new values; and
- Ensures the proper resources are assigned to accomplish the task within budget and schedule.

Role of the Continuous Improvement Coordinator

The primary responsibility of the continuous improvement coordinator is to coordinate the successful implementation of the model line. The supporting responsibilities include the following:

- Coordinates with steering team members;
- Reports status and problem areas to facilitate corrective action when needed;
- Establishes ongoing education program in collaboration with steering team;
- Ensures that teams have a fully developed project plan;
- Supports the teams in using quality improvement processes, applying Just-in Time (JIT) techniques, and developing as a team;
- Aids the team leaders in preparing for meetings, provides feedback on team meetings;
- Provides a link between team leaders and the steering team;
- Keeps up to date on world-class technologies;
- Instructs on general problem-solving techniques;
- Prepares and delivers team training on selected topics, serves as resource person to supervisors, team leaders, and members;
- Monitors progress of the teams, consults on use of techniques;
- Shares experiences and results of team activities with others; and
- Observes group dynamics and works with team leader to design and implement activities that contribute to team health.

Role of the Model Line Team Leader

Duties of the model-line team leader include, but are not limited to, the following:

- Leads the team meetings according to a carefully planned agenda;

- Leads the team through the problem-solving process reflected in the project plan and schedule;
- Teaches/refreshes quality improvement and waste reduction JIT techniques;
- Communicates team progress to the team;
- Communicates/coordinates with supervisor and program coordinator, especially before and after team meetings;
- Shares experience and knowledge;
- Fulfills administrative duties; and
- Encourages team member participation.

Role of the Model Line Team Members

Model-line team members are responsible for:

- Attending all weekly team meetings;
- Identifying opportunities for improvement;
- Participating in selection of items to work on;
- Gathering, prioritizing, and analyzing data;
- Helping the team recommend corrective actions to management;
- Tracking effectiveness of solutions, sharing experience and knowledge;
- Actively participating in team activities;
- Working through the problem-solving process;
- Acting as a recorder when appropriate; and
- Discussing team activities with co-workers who are not team members.

Role of Managers and Supervisors

Managers and supervisors are expected to:

- Ensure that team meetings focus on problems that relate to the objectives of the model line and that members are properly chosen and trained;
- Communicate department objectives to the steering team to aid teams in problem selection;
- Serve as advisors and consultants to the teams, giving them suggestions on possible problem/opportunities to work on;

- Support the functioning of the teams by ensuring that they have necessary resources, such as meeting time, meeting space, materials necessary for smooth operation (data, work schedules, materials), and support of technical resources; and
- Recognize team achievement—provide praise, support, feedback, and continued direction to the teams to reinforce quality achievement and keep the effort alive.

Team Selection and Function

The following criteria should be used for team member selection. Candidates should possess:

- Expertise needed to address problems within the scope of the team;
- A vested interest in the assigned problem area;
- The ability to represent various levels and functions of the organization; and
- The willingness to volunteer and work within a team atmosphere for the length of the project.

Team leaders may be identified by the steering team or selected by team members. Team operational problems (absenteeism, group dynamics, completion of assignments) will be handled collaboratively by team leaders and the program coordinator. Only after all possible avenues for corrective action have been exhausted will the team leader and coordinator ask for assistance from the steering team.

It is strongly recommended that consensus decision making be used in any team problem-solving process. It is a win/win method for team building. Everyone must feel ownership of the action taken.

Regular team presentations (updates) are an opportunity for the team to solicit understanding, support, and approval from management, for the team to experience as a whole all that they have done, and to gain recognition for their activities and accomplishments.

This is part one of the plan. Part two, a time-phased project plan, will be discussed in Chapter 14.

CELEBRATE THE JOURNEY

At a San Francisco company trained in the Lean approach, we talked to the team about how much work it takes to become Lean. One of the team members, let's call him Rob, related a story that summarizes how we must approach the difficult tasks ahead.

Rob was a little overweight and knew that he needed to begin exercising. He decided he would start jogging. Running in San Francisco always means running either uphill or downhill. Rob's route started out with him running uphill. In fact, there was a grade about a mile long behind Rob's house, and every morning he would start out by jogging up this fairly steep grade. As he ran he would focus his eyes on a radio tower at the top of the hill. For the first few days, Rob could only run a short distance before he would have to stop and catch his breath. After dragging himself to the top of the hill, he would walk back home, discouraged that he hadn't been able to run all the way to the top.

After a month, he could run almost to the top before he would begin to tire, but he would push himself on. Closer to the radio tower, his lungs were heaving to pull in air, but he didn't stop. The last part of the hill was steeper than the rest. Rob's legs were burning, screaming for oxygen. Almost to the top, not quite there, he could run no more. He would walk the rest of the way.

This went on for a few more weeks and it seemed that Rob would never be able to make it to the top without stopping. Then one day, the weather had taken a turn for the wet, as it often does in San Francisco. Fog, wind, and rain forced Rob to don a hat. He pulled the baseball cap down low over his face to keep the stinging rain out of his eyes and he started up the hill. He thought about the workday ahead as he plodded along. He thought about the weekend. Every so often he would glance up the hill, but his thoughts returned to the weekend, how badly he needed to clean out the garage, maybe haul some stuff off. His legs were getting tired, but he kept going. The rain was letting up a bit and Rob thought about how he should put some fertilizer on the grass. Then, all the sudden, he looked up and stopped dead in his tracks—at the base of the radio tower. He had made it and he wasn't even very tired. Proud of himself, he took off his hat and threw it into the air.

The next morning, with spirit renewed from the previous day's success, he jumped from bed to look outside. It was a beautiful clear morning. He dressed and sprang out the door. He took a moment to look at the former champion, the radio tower, and then confidently broke into a trot.

Rob was surprised at how quickly he seemed to tire. Not like yesterday's victory at all. Half-way up the hill he was running out of steam. And close to the top he had to give up. He stood bent over, hands to knees, gasping for air as he craned his neck to take a disgusted look at the radio tower. Accepting defeat one more time, he turned and dragged himself home, head hung low, spirit broken again. But not for good.

It took Rob a day or two to figure out what you already have: the morning that he wore a hat, he made the hill easily because he was not focusing on the destination, but on the process.

Most mornings, the radio tower so far away served as a goal. But because of the distance, it also served as a discouragement. When his mind was totally fixated on getting to the top of the hill, thoughts that could make the journey enjoyable were shoved aside. When he wore the hat, it obstructed the view of the hill and he was able to think about other things.

Rob's success was finally possible because he had a clear vision of the goal. The goal did not become an overwhelming or impossible task. It no longer required him to focus all his attention and energy on it, leaving him no time to recharge his mental batteries.

There are similar risks for teams working toward a goal that realistically might be one, two, or three years away. It can be discouraging if they are not allowed to celebrate some milestones along the way. Recognition of progress, however small, is a sign of a well-managed team. Looking back to Chapter One and the Lean enterprise vehicle (the wagon), recall that there are many spokes or techniques that a team can and should apply. Allowing a team to use a model line to implement and practice these techniques is key to proving which techniques work in your environment. The success of a team's applying a particular methodology will have the effect of filling their sails with wind, just as Rob felt when he finally made it to the top of the hill.

Use whatever means possible to get wind in the sails. The team will find plenty of reason for celebrating, but it is hard work, and regular "revival" meetings can prove helpful. Taking teams on a field trip to a customer or vendor using the Lean approach can be profitable for a number of reasons. Getting face to face with customers is always a good way to build a sense of loyalty, responsibility, and ownership in a team that supplies parts to them.

Seeing how other teams have approached a Lean technique is another reason to visit different shops. Seeing success stories and hearing about failed attempts can be more energizing than you would imagine. Recognizing their own progress by seeing areas where they have surpassed other teams is an enormous esteem-booster.

From time to time, sending a member of the team to a Lean workshop or conference can help keep the sails full of wind. If they are sent with the mission to bring back the "goodness" for the rest of the team, it can help them participate in a more intense manner. By the way, this is a great incentive for some people, and it is a way to recognize effort while providing a new experience and chance to interact with other people who are also on the Lean path.

Another way to build enthusiasm is to seek out reading material or video presentations by experts in the field or company owners who have implemented the Lean approach. Such materials can go a long way to show by example the positive effects. Your team will be encouraged to continue the process of building the Lean enterprise.

Construction people can look at blueprints and visualize what the building will look like when it is done. It is a little more abstract for teams trying to build a Lean enterprise. Seeing and hearing the employees at Harley Davidson or Johnsonville Foods can create a hunger to be a part of a group like that. We all need encouragement from time to time, and this process can take years. Keep the sails full.

While filling the sails with wind is important, there is immeasurable cost in allowing ourselves to be blown around by any old wind. "Book-of-the-month" mentalities will quickly kill transformation processes. Projects that are in vogue one day and ignored the next mark the beginning of the end of participation. No one will believe that the organization is truly committed to improvement if the company exhibits a fickle attitude toward projects. If the best efforts and recommendations of project teams are set aside for political reasons, or put on the back burner under the guise of the need for more data collection or more studies, trust will quickly wane and so will the willingness to participate.

Be good at selection. Be good at planning. Be good at executing. Be good at listening. Be good at follow-up and finishing. If you do these things, you will be very, very good!

14

Choose Your Battles Carefully

Firefighters have the most difficult job I can imagine. They have to make dozens of potentially life-effecting decisions everyday. Fighting fires in a building is certainly a formidable task, but fighting against wild fires in nature certainly has some unique and dangerous challenges. These firefighters have to be strategists against all the elements of nature: wind, terrain, and fuel sources of every description. They have to choose when to fight and when to let a fire fight against itself, burning itself out. Knowing when and where to assign firefighters and when to select or de-select a fire are critical skills for those leading the firefighting team. By choosing their battles carefully, the decision-makers keep themselves and those they lead alive.

Carefully choosing your battles at work, while not literally life threatening, could certainly mean the difference between a secure work life and another business fatality. Knowing how and when to assign priorities, and select and de-select projects are powerful and very necessary skills for the executive management team. Once you decide to move forward on a project, stay with it.

SUCCESSFUL TACTICS

There are many ways to get the job done right. We are going to consider the following:

- A lesson from the Civil War,
- Building a time-phased model,
- Strategic planning,
- Using the right tool for the job,
- That every cause needs a leader, and
- The "little brother" effect.

A Lesson from the Civil War

A co-worker once told me that there was a lesson to learn from the Civil War in regard to choosing a battle and staying with it. I am not a Civil War buff, but the analogy he used was powerful and merits discussion. This co-worker and I were talking one day about "staying the course," not allowing ourselves to second-guess the process or to back away from the team's recommendation. He likened the situation we were in to the Civil War. He described how the North had used many different tactics, but were making little headway in fighting the South. The Northern generals and their troops would engage the Southern troops, but when the losses reached a certain threshold, the Northern generals would pull back. Regardless of the potential gain, or that it might have taken only a few more days of fighting for them to win the battle, their approach was to reserve troop numbers, regroup the remnants of the battle, and engage the enemy another day.

Enter General Ulysses Grant. His approach was that, once engaged with the South, he would not back off, regardless of the cost. Because his troops were better equipped, Grant evidently thought that the real ingredient to winning was "time." Wearing down the Southern army meant hitting hard and not letting down for a moment.

Agree or disagree with his approach, the message I received is that we need to be good at finishing. To start a project (battle) and work at it (fight) for a while, only to give up (retreat) in favor of another project or objective (battle), will certainly cost more in the long run, and we could quite possibly lose the war in the process.

Choose your battles carefully. Select those that you know you can win, but even when it hurts, don't back off. It may seem like an uphill battle, but like Rob the runner (discussed in Chapter 13), pull your hat down low and focus on things other than the war. Celebrate the small victories, win enough battles no matter how small, and before you know it, the war is over.

Building a Time-phased Model

Each company is different. The immediate needs of one organization could be viewed as minor by another. There are no templates or one-size-fits-all approaches.

Yet, there are many fundamental steps that seem to be common to each company that I have worked with. This chapter will identify a list of these steps. It is not an all-inclusive list, but a proposed list of items most companies apply as they move from a batch manufacturing system to a Lean manufacturing system. This list represents a complete step-wise approach to successfully applying the Lean enterprise approach to job shops or Original Equipment Manufacturer (OEM) organizations. This book has been about implementing Lean in a job shop environment. Realistically, a large organization with larger resources might take a slightly different approach.

As described earlier, a hybrid approach will work best in the beginning. Start small with a model line and practice until you can bring anyone from anywhere to see how a Lean manufacturing process should look, and how the techniques are applied. Soft link rather than hard link equipment to retain flexibility. You can always hard link later if you decide that it makes economic sense.

Manufacturing teams and the management team need a plan. Chapter 13 showed how the plan could help people understand their responsibilities and accountabilities. This chapter gives an example of a more specific time-phased project plan.

Without a plan, the risk is that we will get busy and another week, month, or year will go by. Just like taking vacation or getting married, if you don't set the date, it won't happen.

The following strategic planning outline may not include every step that should be on your list, but it should help you think about developing your own plan.

Strategic Planning

Specific tasks and goals are part of strategic planning. They can be generalized as follows:

- Phase one —develop the plan,
- Phase two—make sure that you are on the right track, and
- Phase three— —evaluate where you are and decide if any changes are needed to reach the final objective.

Phase One: Develop the Plan

Set up a steering committee.

- Team should be less than five people;
- Team should focus on the large view of things;
- Team should be fairly autonomous and high level;
- Team meetings should be two hours or less per month;
- Purpose of meetings should be to review the strategy;
- Team should have the authority to assign resources to projects once approved by executive management and within the scope of the plan;
- Team must be a self-starting, energized group;
- Team must be able to focus on positive change and on macro-planning rather than have their energy consumed by micro-planning and details; and
- Members must be willing to delegate details to people who can manage them.

Oversee development of an organizational plan to:

- Perform organizational Strength, Weaknesses, Opportunities, and Threats (SWOT) analysis;
- Brainstorm ideas to determine where to start implementing a Continuous Improvement (CI) strategic plan;
- Prioritize ideas;
- Develop aggressive goals; and
- Identify resources.

Assign time frames to accomplish prioritized steps:

- Model line;
- Product, Quantity, Routing, Support Systems, Time (PQRST) data analysis;
- Divide product into value streams;
- Map out product flows (value stream map);
- Identify support machinery capabilities (upstream and down-stream);
- Re-engineer product flows on paper;
- Re-engineer materials management system (pull rather push) future state map;
- Perform setup reduction;

- Develop Takt time for three production levels;
- Develop standard work for three production levels;
- Develop product-specific capacity planning tools for model line;
- Educate teams in use of standard work;
- Virtually link upstream and downstream value streams;
- Develop list of non-value-added activities, and variations, reducing these to a minimum;
- Document new best practices;
- Develop detail layout for machine movements; and
- Physically link equipment(soft link or hard link).

Phase Two: Monitor the Process

- Move to next value stream and repeat the process;
- Develop a Lean promotion office (LPO);
- Develop a system to audit past Kaizen events;
- Develop system to score potential value of a kaizen: does it fit into the long-range kaizen direction (the roadmap)?; calculate payback period;
- Review all Kaizen events concluded within the last year:
  - Identify key players in the organization to lead smaller focused Kaizen teams.
  - Educate the team leaders in: Lean manufacturing principles; Toyota production system; global manufacturing environment; Kaizen formats for setup reduction, waste reduction, elimination of variation, and productivity improvement; facilitation skills; Total Quality Management (TQM) tools of the trade; and Kaizen follow-up skills.
- Develop in-house training and "pay for skill" program.
- Develop "rolling" three-month Kaizen event calendar (high payback or low hanging fruit issues might change this schedule from time to time); and
- Carry out the plan.

Phase Three: Evaluate, Expand, and Revise the Plan

- Redraw the value stream maps to current conditions;
- Identify opportunities for improvement;

- Expand the process described in Phase I to all areas of the shop (and office): scheduling, human resources, accounting, purchasing, and maintenance;
- Develop alternative material handling systems and reduce transportation costs; and
- When program is stable, implement a gain-sharing program.

The Right Tools for the Job

There are many tools at our disposal, as the many spokes on the four wheels of our Lean wagon demonstrate (see Figure 14-1.) Even though it may look like or feel like a buffet, we cannot pick and choose just the items we like. Nor can we select only those techniques that sound easy to implement, or only those methodologies that customers recommend. We must avoid skirting around a section that looks like too much work or that might take us outside of our comfort zone.

A few final suggestions: Find a person who has lived through the adoption of the Lean approach. If possible, have this person join your steering team to offer suggestions and possibly help guide the process. This person could very well be within the walls of

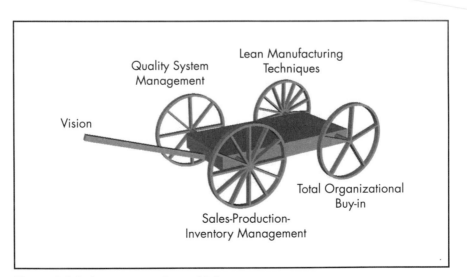

Figure 14-1. Lean enterprise vehicle.

your company right now, an undiscovered diamond. Or, you may find such a person willing and able to help within one of your customers' organizations.

Every Cause Needs a Leader

Every cause needs someone who is willing to be the conscience of the organization, someone willing to go to bat when adequate resources are not being applied to the project as planned. This person needs to be part cheerleader, part drill instructor, part trainer, part coach, part flag waver, part Jiminy Cricket, and part explorer.

Early in the program, find someone in your company to serve as a project coordinator. In very small mom-and-pop shops, this may be Mom or Pop! It may represent a full-time position. The person in this role must be the glue that holds the team together through tough times. It helps if this person has had real-life experience at implementing Lean.

There are at least five or six generations of Toyota production system disciples in the job market today. That means I was taught by someone who was taught by someone who was taught by someone who worked at Toyota. Thus, I became a fourth generation practitioner.

As in any multilevel program, the exponential growth at level six is huge. There is an entire new generation of converts and practitioners out there. Chain letters and multilevel marketing work because if you tell two friends, and they tell two friends, and they tell two friends, mathematically, there is a sound statistical probability that by the time the information gets to the fifth level, there are 63 people with the information.

Chances are there is a disciple or practitioner available in the job market near you who has lived with the Kaizen, JIT, world-class, or Lean approach. Find a person like this to lead the charge and encourage them to be like General Grant: don't let up until the goal is met.

When the progress is not all it should be, the organizational conscience needs to speak frankly and openly. Over time, this can begin to have the sound of a crashing cymbal to the ears of the steering team or executive management. After all, they have many other aspects of the business to manage, not just the application of the Lean approach. Regardless of how much they may believe in the process, there will come a time when other priorities will slow down the progress of the teams. Repeated trips to the woodshed will begin to feel as bad for the one delivering the message as for the ones receiving it, and that is when the "little brother effect" begins.

The Little Brother Effect

What is the "little brother effect?" Have you ever known a family in which the youngest son or daughter is a judge, a doctor, a minister, or a police officer—in other words, a person viewed by society as an authority figure? But within his or her family group, the little brother or sister seldom gets the same respect or attention.

Regardless of a person's skill as a Lean practitioner, once a coordinator has been with a company for a while, he/she will no longer be viewed as the expert. He/she will begin to feel like part of the wallpaper, simply the "little brother," and no one listens to the little brother. Diplomacy and a willingness to confront difficult issues at any level in the organization will therefore be critical characteristics in the hiring criteria for a project coordinator. This is the reason some companies feel compelled to use the services of an outside consultant; someone who is not in the position of becoming the "little brother" and who can take the management team to the woodshed when necessary. An in-house coordinator can do it, but it can be a challenge.

There is an analogy that describes the need for the coordinator to exhibit certain key behaviors and communication skills. In ancient times, shepherds would spend all day guarding and tending to the needs of their flocks. One of the primary tools of the trade was the wooden staff or rod. You may recall the phrase, a parent who "spares the rod, spoils the child." Does that mean that the parent should beat the child? Is that what the shepherds' rod was used for with sheep?

Shepherds took great care to protect their sheep. They certainly didn't beat them. The rod was for self-protection. It was used to ward off the attacks of wolves or other enemies. They used the rod to pry rocks and the curved end as a hook if the need came to retrieve a fallen sheep.

The shepherds also used the rod or staff to direct the sheep. They would guide the sheep with it, first on one side, lightly tapping to indicate the direction the sheep needed to go, then the other side if the sheep went too far. But the rod was never used to abuse or strike the sheep. This is the spirit that the coordinator needs to exhibit with the project teams and with the management teams. A "trip to the woodshed" may therefore create the wrong mental image. These trips must be for the nurturing and coaching of the teams, not for beating up the group.

Time is of the essence. In fact, time *is* the essence. We cannot delay or postpone the changes that are happening worldwide. Dr. W. Edwards Deming, the famed quality guru who helped to turn Japan's quality image around, said it best: "You do not have to do this . . . Survival is not mandatory." But we do want to survive! We do want to be successful! Although it has been repackaged slightly over the last few decades, the Lean approach is not a fad that will go away. Lean techniques and technologies have been added that 10 years ago would have gotten little attention.

The need for becoming Lean is getting more important everyday. Job shops have many unique challenges, but this is no excuse for not being Lean. Economy of scale is often in favor of the small shop. The nimble nature of the mom-and-pop shop can be a major advantage when introducing change.

Outrun your competition by making time your ally instead of your enemy. The first companies to demonstrate competence at being Lean have the opportunity to use it as a marketing tool. Someday everyone will be Lean or they won't be around. Striking early before everyone else is in the game can garner a lot of attention while it is still unique to be Lean. Take advantage of this critical moment in time. Do the right thing for your customers, your employees, your stakeholders, your company, and yourself.

Time is one-directional. Time is irreplaceable. Measure it out as if it were gold dust. Make every second count. Don't stand idly by while it gets spilled out on the floor, piled up in the corner, swept under the rug, or tossed into the dumpster like so much worthless refuse. Infuse your entire organization with this concept: "We will no longer be sharers in the waste of this precious resource. Together we will protect and honor it by using it in a way that shows regard for how limited it is."

Maybe you have played poker before. Poker is what they call a zero-sum game. No more or no less money is available than what is on the table. No matter how long you play, the total amount of money taken home is the same amount everybody started with. If everybody started with $20, and there are five people, then there is $100 available. Regardless of how long the game is played, the amount available will still be $100. This is the principle of a zero-sum game.

Business is also a zero-sum game. There is generally only so much work available, just so many customer orders available, and therefore a limited number of dollars available. To be viewed as good enough to play the game, we must be Lean. Otherwise, the chance is very good that the work will go to someone else who is Lean. If we are going to win this game, we must come to the table ready to play, and prepared to win.

SUMMARY

Anyone who says the Lean approach won't work in a job shop is significantly limiting the potential success of his or her company by shortsighted dinosaur thinking.

The opportunity to learn about the Lean approach and the chance to become a practitioner of this methodology can be the most powerful and rewarding experience of your working life. You don't need to spend thousands of dollars to get started. After a lot of reading and some experimentation, you can learn together and visit other plants. Go to workshops and talk to other companies on the same path. In time, you may turn your manufacturing processes around to align them with the Lean principles. You will also experience the satisfaction of successfully implementing Lean.

Don't let anyone force-fit a template onto your company that they developed at an OEM company. Small companies do not need to and cannot wait three or four years to begin recognizing benefits from the Lean techniques described in this book.

Don't let anyone tell you that you must be a Ford Motor Company, a John Deere, or a Harley Davidson to see the benefits and feel the power that highly enfranchised teams can bring your organization. I encourage you to:

- Be a part of the solution,
- Be a Lean mechanic,
- Be an agent for change,
- Be a flag waver for continuous improvement,
- Be a manager of time,
- Be the best you can be,
- Allow others to be the best they can be,
- Be a horn blower when you see waste,
- Be unbeatable,
- Be an advocate for perfection,
- Be a disciple of Lean within your organization, and
- When you are done . . . pass it on.

Bibliography

Davis, John W. 1999. *Fast Track to Waste-free Manufacturing: Straight Talk from a Plant Manager.* Portland, OR: Productivity Press.

Dettmer, H. William. 1998. *Breaking the Constraints to World-class Performance.* Milwaukee, WI: ASQ Quality Press.

Hammer, Michael, and Champy, James. 1994. *Reengineering the Corporation: A Manifesto for Business Revolution.* New York: Harper Business, May.

Lewis, C. Patrick. 1993. *Building a Shared Vision: A Leaders Guide to Aligning the Organization.* Portland, OR: Productivity Press.

Littauer, Florence. 1992. *Personality Plus.* Tarrytown, NY: F.H. Revell Co.

Miller, William B., and Schenk, Vicki L. 1993. *All I Need to Know About Manufacturing I Learned in Joe's Garage: World Class Manufacturing Made Simple.* Walnut Creek, CA: Bayrock Press.

Muther, Richard, and Wheeler, John D. 1994. *Simplified Systematic Layout Planning,* 3rd ed. Kansas City, MO: Management and Industrial Research Publications.

Peters, Thomas J. 1997. *Circle of Innovation: You Can't Shrink Your Way to Greatness.* New York: Knopf.

Rother, Mike, and Shook, John. 1998, 1999. *Learning to See: Value Stream Mapping to Create Value and Eliminate Muda.* Brookline, NJ: Lean Enterprise Institute.Version 1.1, Version 1.2.

Shingo, Shigeo. 1988. *Nonstock Production: The Shingo System for Continuous Improvement.* Cambridge, MA: Productivity Press.

Shingo, Shigeo. 1989. *Nonstock Production: The Shingo System for Continuous Improvement—A Guide for Group Study.* Cambridge, MA: Productivity Press.

Slater, Robert, and Welch, Jack. 1999. *The GE Way: Management Insights and Leadership, Secrets of the Legendary CEO.* New York: McGraw-Hill.

Suzaki, Kiyoshi. 1987. *The New Manufacturing Challenge: Techniques for Continuous Improvement.* New York: Free Press, Collier Macmillan Publishers.

Womack, James P., and Jones, Daniel T. 1996. *Lean Thinking: Banish Waste and Create Wealth in Your Corporation.* New York: Simon & Schuster.

Zenger, John H., et al. 1994. *Leading Teams: Mastering the New Role.* Homewood, IL: Business One Irwin.

Appendix: Using the CD

The CD-ROM that accompanies this book contains training materials, examples, and samples of some useful tools. These files are based on the Microsoft Office® 97, Small Business Edition, and created in Word®, Excel®, or PowerPoint®. Due to space constraints, only one version of each is stored. If you have older versions of these programs or if you do not have these applications, you will have trouble accessing or importing these files. As an alternative to purchasing a software package, find someone who has the correct version and who can access these files for you, print them out, or save them to a floppy disk in the version you need. Some of the graphics may not transfer when importing them into older formats.

The tools on the CD are given as examples only and will not fit every organization's need. The files are operational and are yours to modify and change. To the best of my knowledge and ability, they have been scanned and are free of any known viruses. I disclaim any responsibility for mistakes, calculation errors, or unknown problems caused by these examples.

The text that follows provides a commentary on some of the charts, samples, and examples on the CD-ROM, as they relate to a particular chapter's topic. Table A-1 gives an outline and commentary on all the material on the CD.

CHAPTER 2

Chapter Two introduces a visual model using a "radar chart." This chart can be accessed in spreadsheet form on the CD-ROM, where you can see a working model and develop your own version. The name of the spreadsheet is: *Fig2-all.xls*.

Table A-1. CD-ROM index of reader-accessible files

Lean Manufacturing Techniques

File Type	File Name	Description	Purpose
Excel	fig6-3.xls	Linearity chart	Spreadsheet allows planner to chart and adjust loaded hours to match available time
Excel	fig7-12.xls	Blank standard work sequence sheet	Allows reader to print out blank form
Excel	fig7-13.xls	Standard work sequence example	Allows reader to follow an example
Excel	fig7-4.xls	Setup observation sheet	Spreadsheet allows reader to experiment with working model of an observation sheet
Excel	form7-1.xls	Time observation form	Blank form allows reader to print out and utilize the time observation technique
Excel	form9-4.xls	Blank precontrol form	Allows the reader to print out and use the precontrol method described in the text
Excel	oee.xls	Overall Equipment Effectiveness (OEE) spreadsheet	Allows reader to view an example and input values to determine OEE
PowerPoint	setuptrn.ppt	Setup reductions	51 slides showing case studies and examples of setup reduction techniques
PowerPoint	valmap.ppt	Value Stream Mapping[SM] presentation	38 slides showing the steps and samples of Value Stream Mapping techniques
PowerPoint	cstdy1.ppt cstdy2.ppt cstdy3.ppt cstdy4.ppt	Setup reduction case studies	Allows readers to view and print out real-life case studies in setup reduction
Excel	product.xls	Productivity spreadsheet	Allows reader to input values to determine labor productivity
Excel	linear.xls	Linearity chart daily hour-by-hour chart	Allows production planners or cell leads to develop

Value Stream Mapping[SM] is a Service Mark of the Lean Enterprise Institute

Table A-1. (continued)

File Type	File Name	Description	Purpose
Excel	smed.xls	Setup observation graph and data	Provides reader with example of setup observation; teams can fill in their data
Excel	takttime.xls	Takt time calculator	Allows teams to calculate takt times for three production levels
Excel	VAratio.xls	Value-added ratio calculator	Allows teams to calculate the value-added ratio of value streams
PowerPoint	fig4-1.ppt	Value stream symbols	After ungrouping these symbols, the reader can cut and paste them into other media
PowerPoint	fig4-4.ppt	Blank value stream map	Allows reader to print out a blank value stream map for use in "walking the process"
PowerPoint	fig7-18.ppt	Facility planning steps	Allows reader to enlarge print size or print out sections for enlargement
Quality System Management			
PowerPoint	5strain.ppt	5-S training	All the slides and forms necessary to provide basic 5-S (sort, straighten, shine, standardize, sustain) team training
Word	intrcspc.doc	SPC training	Presentation for use in Statistical Process Control (SPC) introductory training course
Excel	tab9-3.xls tab9-4.xls	Capability index calculator	Spreadsheet allows reader to enter dimensional data to calculate process capability (C_{PK})
Word	isodoc.doc	ISO documentation workshop	Facilitates training of ISO documentation process

Table A-1. (continued)

File Type	File Name	Description	Purpose
Sales, Production, Inventory Management			
Excel	tab3-3.xls	Product quantity routing worksheet	Allows reader to see examples of how product, quantity, and routing data is entered
Excel	tab3-4.xls	Product quantity routing worksheet	Allows reader to experiment with sorting product, quantity, and routing data
Excel	tab6-1.xls	Economic order quantity (EOQ) spreadsheet	Allows reader to enter data specific to his/her own product and set up cost parameters
Excel	cellcap.xls	Cell capacity planning spreadsheet	Spreadsheet is an aid for the cell planner
PowerPoint	prodsmoo.ppt	Production smoothing	Slides discuss key points of production smoothing
Excel	eoq.xls	Economic order quantity	Allows readers to enter their own data into an EOQ spreadsheet
Excel	tab6-2.xls	Economic order quantity	Spreadsheet allows reader to experiment with economic order quantity data
Total Organizational Buy-in			
Excel	fig10-2.xls	Example gain-sharing spreadsheet	Provides examples of how key business indicators are used in an incentive program
Excel	fig10-3.xls	Example gain-sharing spreadsheet	Provides examples of how key business indicators are used in an incentive program
Excel	fig2-2.xls	Lean enterprise vehicle wheels	Spreadsheet allows the number of spokes and score to be determined for each wheel
Excel	tab10-4.xls	Performance-based wage worksheet	Allows the reader to experiment with different wage structures and job criteria
PowerPoint	safetrn.ppt	Safety training	Slides facilitate the training of safety instructors

Table A-1. (continued)

File Type	File Name	Description	Purpose
PowerPoint	vision.ppt	Organizational vision presentation	Slides outline approach to get from organizational vision to value stream mapping
PowerPoint	citrain.ppt	Training for Kaizen teams	All the slides and forms necessary to provide basic Kaizen team training
PowerPoint	Leantrng.ppt	Full-day Lean manufacturing training	All slides and simulation for day-long training in Lean principles
PowerPoint	leadtrng.ppt	12-week leadership training	250 slides/36-hour course (3 hours/week) for teaching teamwork skills
Word	intrview.doc	Training interview	Format for developing training outlines through interviews with expert operators
Excel	fig2-all.xls	Wagon-wheel radar charts	Shows readers the individual spokes of the "business" wagon wheel and allows them to enter their own labels and data
Excel	leader.xls	Leadership selection criteria	Teams can use this spreadsheet to objectively choose a leader
Excel	projsel.xls	Project selection spreadsheet	Spreadsheet allows reader to use weighted values to determine project viability
Excel	teamsurv.xls	Team survey	Facilitates evaluation of team member characteristics
PowerPoint	enfranch.ppt	Enfranchisement slides	Slides detail change process
PowerPoint	leanun.ppt	Lean enterprise training	Slides provide a modular approach to Lean training
Word	form 2-1.doc	Leadership continuum	Shows the phases of team development and allows reader to enter their own data
PowerPoint	kpo.ppt	Kaizen promotion office plan	Slides give instruction on how to set up a Kaizen promotion office

CHAPTER 3

Table 3-1 of Chapter Three shows a Product Quantity Routing spreadsheet, which is used to start the process of sorting product families and value streams. Sample spreadsheets are titled: *Tab3-3.xls* and *Tab3-4.xls*.

CHAPTER 5

Chapter Five discusses the calculation of value-added versus non-value-added ratios. One way to express the value-added ratio is to calculate what percentage of lead time is value-added and what percentage is non-value-added. The spreadsheet titled *Varatio.xls* will perform these calculations.

CHAPTER 6

Chapter Six refers to a team training exercise that shows the advantage of a one-piece flow system as compared to a batch manufacturing system. This training is on the CD-ROM as a slide presentation. The slides can be printed out or modified for use in training. The file name is *Leantrng.ppt*.

A building toy, available in toy stores, is used in the training to simulate the manufacturing or assembly process, as shown in Figure 6-1. You can purchase the various sizes described in the simulation at most toy stores, modify the suggested product, or create your own simulation. If you wish to use the exact exercise described, you will need to purchase multiple kits to obtain all the pieces necessary for the exercise. For example, to build one exercise kit with 16 sets of each color, four Lego™ kits (No. 1776/950 pieces) were purchased. Then, the specific pieces needed were separated.

The linearity charts shown in Figures 6-2 and 6-3 are in the spreadsheet titled: *Linear.xls*. Instructions for use are included on its first page.

A spreadsheet to make the cost of setups more visual while using the Economic Order Quantity (EOQ) graph is titled *EOQ.xls*. It can be used as is or modified to reflect cost parameters, such as unit cost, planning cost, or setup costs at a plant.

During an observation of setup activities, discussed in Chapter 6, one team member keeps track of time with a stopwatch. The spreadsheet titled *Fig7-1.xls* will perform the time calculations for each activity.

The linearity charts discussed in Chapter 6 are available on the CD-ROM as *Linear.xls*. They also can be used to monitor productivity against planned goals. The spreadsheet includes a chart for measuring waste rates.

CHAPTER 7

Chapter Seven discusses setup reduction processes. Some case studies of setup reduction projects are included on the CD-ROM. The files are in four separate slide presentations titled: *Cstudy1.ppt*, *Cstudy2.ppt*, *Cstudy3.ppt*, and *Cstudy4.ppt*.

Takt time is used to set the rhythm or pace for a manufacturing process. A spreadsheet is given for calculating Takt time, titled *Takttime.xls*. The spreadsheet can be copied as is or modified.

A cycle time observation sheet, to be used while developing standard work time, is available on the CD ROM. It is titled *Form7-12.xls*.

A setup observation form is available as a spreadsheet. The title is *Form7-1.xls* (Table 7-8).

A standard work combination sheet (shown in Figures 7-11 and 7-12) is available in spreadsheet form. There are two files: *Fig7-11.xls* and *Fig7-12.xls*.

The steps for facility planning, shown in Figure 7-17, are available as *Fig 7-18.ppt*. This can be printed out to any desired scale for ease of reading.

CHAPTER 9

The International Organization for Standardization's quality standard, ISO 9000, is discussed in Chapter Nine. Copies of Figures 9-9 and 9-10 and many other documents related to an ISO 9000 program can be found in *isosamp.doc*. Companies in the process of developing an ISO system may find these documents helpful. Intended as examples of what other companies have done, the samples may not fit your company's needs. They should not be used to develop organization policy manuals, procedures, or work instructions.

Samples of the pre-control charts are in *Form9-4.xls*.

A spreadsheet is included on the CD-ROM that performs the C_{PK} calculations to assist in identifying the capability index for your machines. The files are titled *Tab9-3.xls* and *Tab9-4.xls*.

CHAPTER 10

A spreadsheet with sample wages and calculations for scoring the physical, mental, and technical demand of a job is titled *Tab10-4.xls*. Job titles can be changed, if desired. The spreadsheet is protected by the password "wage," should any formulas need to be changed.

An example of a gain-sharing program made visible and measurable is titled *Fig10-2.xls*. The items measured and the values entered can be changed by selecting the "unprotect sheet" function (under the "tools" pull-down menu) in the spreadsheet. The password is "gainshare."

CHAPTER 11

An interview with key points for talking with an expert is given in the file titled *Intrview.doc*.

CHAPTER 12

The team enfranchisement continuum, used to assist in moving teams toward independence and responsibility, is available in *Form12-1.doc*.

A sample of the spreadsheet showing the team leadership selection process is titled *Leader.xls*.

Index

CD-ROM INSTALLATION INSTRUCTIONS

Recommended Requirements: Hardware: PII or better CPU with sound card; 10 MB or more of available hard-disk space; 8× CD drive or faster; 800 × 600 screen resolution, 256 colors or more. *Operating System:* Microsoft Windows® 9X or later. *Memory:* 16 MB, 32 or more preferred. *Internet Access:* Internet Explorer® 5.0 or later, Netscape® 4.7 or later. *Software*: Microsoft Office® '97.

Insert the CD into your CD-ROM drive. The CD will automatically play.